Alive and Aware

Alive and Aware
Improving Communication in Relationships

Sherod Miller, Ph.D.
Elam W. Nunnally, Ph.D.
Daniel B. Wackman, Ph.D.

ISBN 0-917340-01-9 (cloth)
ISBN 0-917340-02-7 (paper)
First Printing, October, 1975,
Second Printing, July, 1976,

Design: Robert Friederichsen
Typesetting: Computer Graphics, Inc.
Printing: Printing Arts Inc.
Printed on Recycled paper.

INTERPERSONAL
COMMUNICATION PROGRAMS, INC.

300 Clifton Avenue
at The Carriage House
Minneapolis, Minnesota 55403

PREFACE

If you lived for any length of time with both of your parents, no doubt you saw them make decisions together: what food to eat, how much money to spend, what to do with a free evening, what clothes to wear, or maybe just who would walk through a door first. But *if you're over 18*, the odds are great against having seen your parents talk together about how they typically made decisions or talk openly about any differences they had in their relationship to better their relationship. In short, few people have seen their parents talk about how they talk.

If your parents learned their lessons well while they were growing up, they wouldn't think of such talk. To over simplify a bit, back then roles were set—there's a man's role and a woman's role and when everyone's doing what they're supposed to do, there are no problems.

But in today's world, roles and relationships are no longer as clearly defined as they once were. Relationships are becoming more complex with a variety of opportunities for relating. Roles are changing and new ones are being created. In this new situation, where role-making rather than role-taking is becoming the norm, a new consciousness and communication skills become important.

Until recently, if you and your partner (at work, a friend, or mate) wanted to enhance and develop your relationship, you had no alternative for doing so without declaring that one or both of you were having serious problems and needed a consultant/counselor to help out. And then, if you did see a consultant/counselor while you worked on "your problem," s/he probably spent little or no time teaching you principles and skills for solving future difficulties on your own, without his/her aid. So, both at home and elsewhere, limited help was available to assist you in "learning to learn" in relationships or in enriching your partnerships by effectively talking about how you talk.

Now there are alternatives available—this book is one of them. You don't have to have a problem to qualify either, only a desire to improve the quality of your life with someone important to you—a wish to make something good even better.

In ALIVE AND AWARE we have tried to share what we know about modern communication along with principles and specific behavioral skills for helping you and your partner communicate more effectively together.

ACKNOWLEDGEMENTS

Unfortunately, most people who read ALIVE AND AWARE will never have the opportunity to know the people who have contributed personally to the creation of this book. These are significant people for us:

Reuben Hill, Former Director of the University of Minnesota Family Study Center, currently Regents Professor of Sociology. Spending time with Reuben is an uplifting experience. He was the first to introduce us to the notion of "relationship development" in the mid-1960s. As Principal Investigator of the NIMH Family Problem-Solving Grant, he's been the key person, intellectually and financially, in support of our research.

Earl Beatt, Director of Minneapolis Family and Children's Service. Earl became excited about translating developmental theory into practice, and supported us generously with agency staff, time, and money.

William Fawcett Hill, Professor of Psychology, California State Polytechnic (Pomona). Bill provided us with the first framework on communication that really made sense—the Hill Interaction Matrix. It distinguishes *what* is said from *how* something is said.

Sidney M. Jourard, the late Professor of Psychology, University of Florida. More than anyone we've met, Sidney was committed to self-disclosure and to waging war on fraud and deceit in relationships. His accidental death, while we were writing this book, is still an enormous shock and loss to us. He was going to write a foreword to our book.

Virginia Satir, Family Therapist and Educator, Palo Alto, California. Virginia is a constant source of ideas. She likes to think of herself as a "yeasting" person, generating ideas and possibilities for others to develop. From Virginia, we've learned a great deal about process and congruence.

Phyllis Miller, Eeva Nunnally and *Kathy Wackman*, our wives. Phyllis, Eeva, and Kathy are the most significant people in our lives. Both working and playing with them has contributed immensely to keeping this a practical book.

Ramon Corrales, Associate Director of the Family Study Center, University of Missouri, and *James W. Maddock*, Education and Training Coordinator for the Program in Human Sexuality, University of Minnesota Medical School. Ramon and Jim are friends and colleagues. They have contributed and refined ideas presented in ALIVE and AWARE.

David and *Vera Mace*, Co-founders of Association of Couples for Marriage Enrichment; *Nena* and *George O'Neill*, Authors of *Open Marriage* and *Shifting Gears*; and *Michael Paula*, Pioneer for Human Growth, Hamburg, Germany. Each of these people have enriched our understanding of relationship development.

Ron Brazman, Psychotherapist, Minneapolis, Minnesota, and *Peggy Granger*, Editor, Science and Behavior Books. Both Ron and Peggy made valuable contributions to the writing and editing of this book.

Lastly, we want to thank the Couple Communication Instructors, participants, and students who freely shared their ideas, experiences, and transcripts with us.

CONTENTS

1. Alive and Aware: A Perspective on Relationships 11

SECTION I. SELF-AWARENESS
2. The Awareness Wheel 29
3. Disclosing Self-Awareness 53
4. Complete and Congruent Self-Awareness 79

SECTION II. AWARENESS OF OTHER
5. To Share A Meaning 103
6. What We Talk About 130
7. Understanding/Misunderstanding;
   Agreement/Difference 148

SECTION III. STYLES OF COMMUNICATION
8. Three Styles of Communication 173
9. Style IV: A Committed Style 197
10. Mixed Messages 212

SECTION IV. PATTERNS OF COMMUNICATION
11. Building Self and Other Esteem 223
12. Contracting to Work on an Issue 246
13. Trouble Shooting: What Can Go Wrong and How to
    Deal With It 260

14. Postscript: Communication and Relationships 279
Appendix: What is Couple Communication? 285
Index 286

CHAPTER ONE

ALIVE AND AWARE

Almost everyone is talking about improving relationships these days, and for good reason. Relationships give life a depth of meaning provided by few other human experiences. They offer the potential for enormous gain in a person's individual growth and enjoyment of life. At the same time, they may—and perhaps too often do—hinder growth and enjoyment of life.

Another reason people are talking a lot about improving relationships is that there is little in our culture that teaches us how to nurture relationships so we can realize their full potential. In fact, too often the relationships we experience emphasize manipulation and exploitation. Frequently, parents manipulate children and each other; children exploit their peers; teachers use their students; students use their teachers; politicians manipulate the public. Television is crawling with exploitive relationships.

Because relationships are so important, and because the examples of them that our culture provides are often unrewarding and unsatisfying, many people are not only talking about them, but are also becoming concerned about improving the quality of relationships. As a consequence, lots of books are being written about how to do it. Why should anyone want to write another one? Aren't there enough good ones already?

We think not. A number of these books prescribe what a good relationship should be. But who can really say what is best for you? Other books provide advice on what you can do specifically to make your relationship better. Although some of this advice may be helpful to you, too often the advice is so specific that it doesn't fit situations arising in your own relationship. Some books provide a relatively integrated approach you can use to improve your relationships. This approach is generally more helpful, but frequently the ideas presented are too abstract to apply effectively in your relationships.

In this book, we present an *integrated approach* to improving relationships. What we think is different about our approach is that we present a variety of *specific communication skills* you can use in most of your relationships. The communication skills you can learn from this book provide you with more effective tools for examining your relationships, and for changing them if you choose. With these skills you can increase your capability and your flexibility in communicating with others and, as a consequence, increase your ability to choose the shape and direction of your relationships.

As you progress through ALIVE AND AWARE, you will be introduced to a number of frameworks for thinking about communication. Connected to each of the frameworks are skills which enable you to use these frameworks in communicating with others. You will find that these frameworks come to life and help your communication as you use the related skills.

Before we focus directly on the communication frameworks and skills, we'd like to provide you with an overview of relationships.

A FRAMEWORK FOR LOOKING AT RELATIONSHIPS

The word "relationship" means lots of different things to different people. For example, the President of the United States might use the word to describe what goes on between himself and the voters. Other people restrict their use of the word to very intimate relationships, such as those between lovers or parent and child. For us, two people have a relationship when they have a history together and anticipate some kind of future; that is, when they have ongoing expectations for each other. In our terms, casual acquaintances wouldn't have a relationship, nor would a sales person and a customer in a store. When we use the term "relationship," we're thinking of more potentially significant ties between people, such as those between a supervisor and an employee, student and teacher, professional colleagues, business partners, roommates, close friends, and, of course, husband and wife, and parent and child.

Because we're talking about so many different pairs of people, we've decided to call two members of a relationship "partners." Whether you are a wife or husband, parent or child, boy friend or girl friend, friends—two men or two women together—what you have in common with the other person in the pair is that you are both partners. And as partners, both of you share the responsibility for what happens in your relationship.

We're going to describe several relationship *states*, that is, specific postures partners adopt toward each other. Partners can be in a relationship state for just a brief moment, a longer interval, or for a considerable length of time—perhaps even years. There is no general pattern of how long a particular relationship state may continue within a partnership.

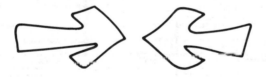

We distinguish four specific relationship states. We call the first one *togetherness*. In this state, partners are involved with each other, sharing, caring, playing, talking seriously about an issue in their relationship, or perhaps arguing or fighting. The key point here is that both partners are focusing their involvement and energies on each other or the same thing. Togetherness is very often seen in newly-formed relationships, although not exclusively so. New friendships, new marriages, new partnerships of any kind often begin in a state of togetherness. Parents may feel a strong togetherness watching their child take the first few steps or graduate from college. Business partners may be in a state of togetherness after finalizing an important contract. These are both examples of togetherness states involving pleasant feelings. But partners can be in a state of togetherness with bad feelings too, for example, when a husband and wife argue about a purchase, or roommates disagree over housekeeping responsibilities.

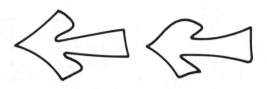

We label the second relationship state a *leading/supporting* state. This state occurs when one partner takes the lead, choosing to focus his/her energies on some outside interest or activity, and the second partner follows lending encouragement and support. The classic example of the leading/supporting state occurs in traditional marriages where the man develops his career, encouraged and supported by the woman. However, there are many other examples in everyday life. For example, a partner makes all the arrangements for an evening's entertainment, or one partner takes care of the children, while the other partner attends a conference out of town. If the second partner's support and encouragement is strong, positive feelings for both partners usually occur, but if it is only a grudging support, negative feelings often result.

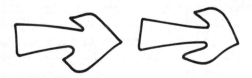

We label the third relationship state a *pushing/resisting* state. This occurs when one partner prods or pressures the second into focusing his energy in a certain direction. As with the other states, either positive or negative feelings can arise. If, for example, the prodding is rather gentle and the activity is rewarding, good feelings are likely to result for both partners. More often though heavy pressure is applied by the first partner and the activity is not rewarding resulting in strong negative feelings and resistance.

The classic example of this state again occurs in marriages, where the "strong" partner pushes the "weak" partner to success. But this state too has many common everyday examples, such as, the parent prodding a child into activities, a supervisor suggesting an employee do a certain task and so forth.

It should be pointed out that either partner can play the leader role in the leading/supporting state, and either can play the pressuring role in the pushing/resisting state. As a consequence, for any relationship there are really two leading/supporting states, i.e., partner A leading and B supporting, and partner B leading, A supporting. Similarly, any relationship can have two pushing/resisting states, i.e., partner A pushing and B resisting, and partner B pushing with A resisting.

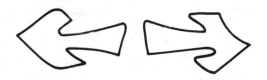

The fourth relationship state we label *apartness*. As the word suggests, it is almost the opposite of togetherness. Apartness occurs when partners are focusing their involvement and energies away from each other or on different things. Examples of this state can be found everywhere: when a husband and wife pursue their own separate careers, or when roommates maintain separate circles of friends. A state of apartness can be pleasant and comfortable or upsetting, just as we found with the other states. When the husband and wife pursuing separate careers do so in an encouraging, supportive fashion, apartness is likely to be very fulfilling for each partner. But if one of them views the other's career as an indication of disinterest or lack of commitment to their relationship, apartness is likely to be painful or threatening.

Figure 1-1 Possible States of a Relationship.

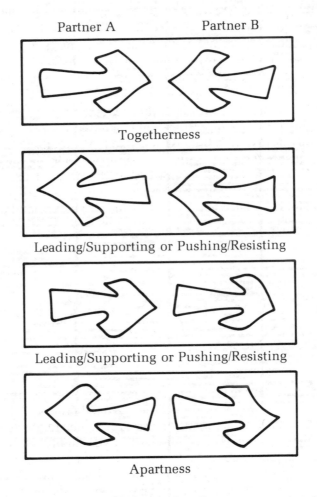

Partner A   Partner B

Togetherness

Leading/Supporting or Pushing/Resisting

Leading/Supporting or Pushing/Resisting

Apartness

To summarize our discussion briefly, at any point in time, relationships can be viewed as being in one of four states: togetherness, leading/supporting, pushing/resisting, or apartness. For the second and third states, two variants are possible, depending on the role each partner plays. The possible states for any relationship are shown in Figure 1-1.

Your Relationship Around Issues.

The relationship framework can be used to look at a number of different aspects of your relationship. First, let's see how it can be applied when a partnership deals with a specific issue such as leisure time. Partners who share all leisure activities have a togetherness pattern, whereas those who share none have an apartness pattern. Relationships in which one partner does all the planning and organizing of leisure activities may be in a leading/supporting pattern if the second partner goes along with most activities, or a pushing/resisting pattern if the second partner generally resists.

Few partnerships fill their leisure time using only one state, of course. Rather, some activities, such as going to parties, camping, boating, or eating supper often involve togetherness, and others, such as reading, meditating, or doing a hobby usually involve apartness. Sometimes one partner leads and the other follows, and at other times the roles are switched. At other times still, one partner may push the second into new activities, and again the roles may be switched. In fact, many partnerships are likely to involve all of these states at one time or another in utilizing their leisure time.

Think about a partner of yours for a moment. Who comes to mind? Whether your partner is a spouse, a steady guy or gal, or a close friend of the same sex, think about how the two of you deal with your leisure. What percent of the time are the two of you in a state of togetherness? Of apartness? Of leading/supporting? Of pushing/resisting? When you and your partner are in the leading/supporting state, who usually leads? How about the pushing/resisting state—who usually does the pushing?

Let's take another issue—work activities. For married partners, if both are working outside the home or only one is, responsibilities have to be allocated and tasks performed, such as paying bills, household chores, shopping, and child care if there are children. But for non-married partners, time allotted to work activities has to be allocated, too. For example, student partnerships have to decide how study time is to be decided upon and roommates have to determine how household tasks are to be performed. So whatever the basis of your relationship with your partner, the two of you have to make decisions regarding some aspect of your work activities.

What kinds of decisions have you and your partner made? Think about one of your work activities, such as housework, child care, studying, and so forth. What percent of the time do you and your partner spend in this activity in a state of togetherness? Of apartness? Of leading/supporting, or of pushing/resisting? Who usually is leading and who usually is pushing?

YOUR RELATIONSHIP OVER TIME.

You can take other areas of your relationship and examine them with the relationship framework, too. The framework can also be used in another way. You can use it to take an overall look at your partnership over a period of time. Let's look at two rather long periods of time first.

John and Elaine have been married for 30 years. Throughout much of this period, John focused most of his energy on building his automobile dealership. He joined a variety of civic organizations and a church, assuming a number of leadership positions. John and Elaine's social contacts grew largely out of the many people John met through his business and organization connections. During this period, Elaine organized much of her life around John's career. In the last few years, with their children grown up, Elaine has become actively involved in local politics, serving once as campaign manager for a friend. These activities have created some tensions between John and her. However, since John's shifting of a number of responsibilities to others at the dealership, there has been a greater sharing of activities. Now Elaine plans to run for the city council with John as her campaign manager.

This story is a true one, and it is characteristic of many late middle-aged marriages in this country. For many years, the basic relationship state is that of leading/supporting with the husband leading. As the children grow up, the wife becomes involved in new activities, resulting in an apartness state for several years, or perhaps for the rest of their marriage. Finally, when the husband begins to cut back on his work, the couple can shift to a general state of togetherness, sharing many of their activities.

Let's move ahead a generation now and look at John and Elaine's son Mike. Mike is a senior in college and has been living with Carol for the past year. Carol is a first year graduate student, working on a

Master's degree in speech therapy. They do most of their studying together in their apartment, and they spend much of their leisure time with a small group of friends, but both also have separate jobs, friends and participate in separate activities. Mike plays banjo with a group two nights a week, and Carol is a part-time debate coach at a junior college. At various times during their two and one-half year relationship each has pushed the other to consider marriage, but they haven't both wanted to do so at the same time. They intend to continue living together, but both of them have ruled out marriage in the meantime.

Carol and Mike's relationship generally can be viewed as involving a great deal of togetherness and some apartness. At different times in their relationship, a pushing state developed as first one and then the other pushed for marriage. This created some tension in their relationship when it occurred, but the overall result has been to help them clarify their individuality and their relationship. They both feel comfortable in sharing much of their lives together, yet at the same time, keeping important parts of their lives apart.

Think about your own partnership again for a moment. Look at it from the time you began to feel attracted to your partner. Have you generally been in a single relationship state during most of this period, or have you moved from one state to another? At various points in time during your relationship, have you shifted frequently between two or more states? Which ones? Thinking about the whole period of your relationship, when have you been most comfortable with it? When have you been least comfortable?

YOUR RELATIONSHIP AND TIME.

A third way to use the relationship framework is similar to the second, but focuses on a much shorter period of time. When you use it this way, you look at your relationship for a day, a couple of days, or perhaps a week. Let's look again at Mike and Carol and see what happens in their relationship during a typical day.

They get up at the same time and have breakfast together. Carol leaves first for an early class, and Mike stays in their apartment studying. Late in the morning, she returns home and they spend a half hour studying together before lunch. Frequently they lunch together before Mike leaves for his afternoon classes. Carol also leaves soon to meet with her debate team, then returns to the apartment before Mike. Mike shops for groceries on the way back from class. They fix dinner together, then begin studying. About 9:30, they finish their work and drop over to a friend's house to finish the day.

During this day, Mike and Carol have been in a state of togetherness at a number of different times, and their overall pattern for the day is basically togetherness. However, each has pursued his own activities too, resulting in several states of apartness during the day. Further, at times even when they have been together physically, they have been in a state of apartness as they did their separate school work. During the day, they did not experience either the leading/supporting or pushing states, although Carol had to coax Mike a bit to go grocery shopping. For Mike and Carol, this day was a comfortable one as they shifted from one relationship state to another.

How about you and your partner? Think of a recent day in your partnership. What states were you in during this day? How frequently did you shift from one to the other? How easy were the shifts to make? Did you experience discomfort when the two of you were in any particular state?

VIABLE AND LIMITING RELATIONSHIPS.

We think the relationship framework is useful in all these ways for helping you to focus on your relationship. We hope you found it helpful, too. We don't think any single pattern is ideal for a relationship. Rather, we think each partnership has to find the mix that both partners find most comfortable. Nevertheless, we do think that moving, growing, viable relationships include all of these states at different times. Togetherness and apartness, leading and supporting, pushing and resisting all are essential for a growing relationship. Relationships which rotate primarily between the states of togetherness and apartness are typically productive and happy ones. But even these relationships shift to the leading/ supporting and pushing/resisting states in order to introduce new experiences and new information, and discover new possibilities.

In contrast to viable relationships there are limiting ones. Limiting relationships may have many satisfactions for partners, but we've chosen to call them "limited" because one or more of the relationship states is missing, or is not permitted. Maybe a husband is not allowed to push the wife. Perhaps partners are locked into one state, for example, continuous togetherness. Other relationships we've seen look like revolving doors, with partners taking turns pushing each other. Whenever one state is missing, no matter which one, a limitation is placed on the relationship because the possibility of using the new experiences of one or both partners is reduced.

By looking at your relationship in a number of ways, using the relationship framework, you can increase your awareness of what patterns you have had in the past and what your present patterns are. But if you want to make changes in your relationship patterns, or use your relationship more effectively for your own personal growth and that of your partner you need more than simply an awareness of these patterns. You also need tools to help build the kind of relationship you and your partner want. We think the most effective tools available for this purpose are your communication skills.

COMMUNICATION FRAMEWORKS AND SKILLS.

The rest of this book focuses on communication skills. It does this by first presenting a framework for examining a specific aspect of interpersonal communication, then introducing you to a set of skills which will help you improve that part of your own communication.

The first section introduces you to the *Awareness Wheel*, a framework which will help you identify the various kinds of information you have inside yourself. Connected to the Awareness Wheel are six specific skills to help you communicate this self-information more completely and congruently.

The second section introduces you to the *Shared Meaning Process* and the skills you can use to more effectively tune into your partner and help him/her tune into you. This section also introduces you to a framework for thinking about the content of interpersonal communication and the kinds of issues involved in ongoing relationships.

The third section describes *Verbal Communication Styles* and shows how the various skills discussed earlier fit together and can be used in an integrated fashion.

The fourth section discusses a framework of particular importance for building relationships—the *I Count/I Count You* framework. We think this framework is especially important because we know that relationships cannot be built simply by applying specific skills. Rather, relationship building requires a spirit as well as skills, and the spirit needed is effectively captured by this framework. This section also describes a specific process partners can use to seriously examine an issue in their relationship—the mini-contract. And the section concludes with a chapter discussing what can be done when communication breakdowns occur.

A final chapter returns the focus to relationships, discussing the connections between the relationship framework and the various communication frameworks and skills presented in the book.

WHO IS THE BOOK FOR?

This book is written for anyone interested in improving his or her relationships. Our experiences indicate that people who learn some of the frameworks and skills presented in the book, and use them in their daily lives, gain greater satisfaction from their relationships.

The widespread concern about relationships probably is based on a much broader concern in our society today—a concern for improving the quality of life generally. Such diverse ways as the ecology movement, interest in yoga and transcendental meditation, consumer protection movement, support for minority and women's rights, and interpersonal relations capture these concerns most directly.

New life styles, new patterns of communal living, and the increase in the numbers of couples living together without being married are dramatic examples of this concern—by no means restricted to young people. Such concerns are also reflected in the increasing numbers of couples of all ages who participate in growth experiences, see counselors, or try to improve their relationship by themselves. The concern extends far beyond male/female relationships. Even the increasing divorce rate can be viewed as a quest for quality of relationships. Four out of five people who divorce eventually remarry,[1] and half of these people remarry within the first year of their divorce.

There is one kind of relationship, however, in which these communication skills are not appropriate, not helpful. That is in a structured, competitive relationship. Here we mean situations in which two people are competing for something which both cannot have. Common examples of these structurally competitive relationships are labor management negotiations or adversary proceedings in court. In structurally competitive relationships, withholding of information is often crucial to success, so the use of these skills is counter-productive. Most of the skills presented in this book are useful for increasing the information partners share with each other so we think you will find it advisable not to use these skills in such situations. We'll point out specific instances when you might want to stay away from these skills at various points in the book.

However, there is another kind of competitive situation in which these communication skills are relevant and helpful—namely, when partners in what is basically an intimate, cooperative relationship compete with one another. The relationship becomes temporarily competitive because the partners define it that way. For example, two children often compete for the same friend. Yet this competition is really unnecessary because all three can be friends at the same time. Similarly, adults will often turn a cooperative situation into a competitive one, for example, when they argue about whose plan is "right" or "better" instead of attempting to reconcile the two. In these situations, our experience indicates that these communication skills can be extremely helpful in changing competition into cooperation, paving the way for further development of the relationship.

---

[1]Paul C. Glick, "A Demographer Looks at American Families," *Journal of Marriage and the Family*, 37, No. 1 (February 1975): 15-26.

HOW TO READ THIS BOOK

We think you'll find this book loaded with information. In fact, we may have included too much! But we don't think this is a book that should—or could—be read once and totally understood and assimilated. Why? Because much of what can be learned from the book will not be learned, in fact, until you begin using the ideas in your daily life. This is especially true of the communication skills; as with any other skills, you can only learn them by using them. Reading about the skills is not enough. So as you read, experiment with the skills you are learning about; maybe select just one from a section and try to use it in your relationship before moving to the next section. After you begin to feel comfortable using the skill regularly, select a second one and experiment with it. You might want to move into the next section at this point. After reading this section, again select a single skill and practice using it.

You can do the same thing with the frameworks presented in this book. Use them to look at your relationships and your communication with your partner. Use the frameworks to reflect back on situations when the two of you communicated effectively. Do the same for situations when your communication wasn't effective. At various points in the book we try to help you use the frameworks by asking you to stop reading for a time and think about your relationship. We have done this several times in this chapter. We think the frameworks will mean much more to you if you take these pauses seriously and use them to examine your relationships.

We think you can learn a great deal about communication skills and frameworks if you read the book slowly and try to make the skills a part of your daily life. Perhaps you already have learned a number of these skills. If so, take the opportunity to practice and refine them as you read along. For either learning or refining these skills, we urge you to read the book and practice the skills with your partner. Again, our experience indicates that partners help each other learn the frameworks and skills, particularly by helping each other practice the skills regularly. So if you have the chance, try to read ALIVE AND AWARE with your partner.

Whether you already have these skills or not, we think you should be aware that you will not be able to use them effectively overnight. It takes a long time to become skillful in anything, and communication is no exception. Although some of the skills may be difficult to learn, and it will take some time to learn all of them, we know that you can. We know this because almost everyone who has participated in the program this book is based on has learned some skills. And many have learned most of the skills, even though the program lasts only four weeks.

When you have learned the frameworks and skills and made them a part of your life, we think you'll find your relationship more satisfying. New horizons will appear for you and your partner. You will be able to use your experiences to build your relationship. In short, you'll find that the options for your relationship will multiply, and you and your partner will be able to effectively make choices for the direction you want your relationship to go, perhaps for the first time. When this happens—when you are aware of yourself, your partner, and your relationship —your relationship will come alive.

SECTION I

SELF-AWARENESS

The first step in all communication is identifying information you want to communicate to others. In interpersonal communication, this information is often information about yourself, yet frequently people have a great deal of trouble identifying all the kinds of information they have about themselves.

The chapters in this section are about self-awareness, about the wealth of information each person has about him/herself. They will discuss ways to better identify self-information, and skills you can use to disclose this awareness more completely and congruently.

CHAPTER TWO

THE AWARENESS WHEEL

"What's happening now?"

What's happening to you right now? What are you sensing? Thinking? Feeling? Wanting? Doing? If you are a living, breathing person, all these dimensions are very active. They're telling you what's happening on the inside of you and on the outside of you. They're letting you know the condition that your own world is in. And when you're with your partner, you each get lots of messages about the state of your relationship.

Many people complain that their partner doesn't "communicate," but unless that non-communicator is in a coma, it is just not true. When you and your partner are together, it's impossible for the two of you not to communicate. You don't believe that? Watch Pam and Jack studying for exams in Pam's apartment:

> Pam looks up from her book, and says, "Jack, let's take a break now. Maybe go over to Cicero's and get a pizza. Want to?"
>
> Jack grunts, but continues to read. Pam moves over next to him and scratches the back of his neck, "Are you ready to take the break now?" Jack doesn't reply and continues to read.

Maybe the most important thing Jack will learn during this study session and which you can also learn as an onlooker, is that even his silence communicates. But for Pam, the problem is how to unscramble the silent coded message. Does Jack mean, "Go away and leave me alone?" Or does he mean, "Wait until I finish reading this page." Or perhaps he means, "Coax me a little more," or maybe even, "You know I don't like pizza, I'm going to hang tight until you suggest hamburgers." Pam will make some choice, draw some conclusions about Jack's intentions. With some luck (every now and then) in a situation like this, she'll guess right.

The question for Jack though, is this: does he really want to give up his choice of the message Pam receives? Does he even know some of the messages his silence might be giving her. Jack's silence is saturating the relationship with messages. But his messages may or may not be heard by Pam as he intends. Jack can *choose* to communicate only information of which he is aware, and he can tell whether or not Pam gets his message accurately only if he's aware of her responses.

Maintaining awareness about "what's happening right now" is a process of gathering and identifying information about yourself, your partner, and your interaction together. The first order of business in this and the next chapter is to find out how we can maintain awareness of ourselves. When we are in contact with our own awareness, then we can communicate our own thoughts, feelings, intentions, and actions more effectively. From here we can expand our awareness of our partner and our relationship. That will be the concern of later chapters.

THE AWARENESS WHEEL: MAINTAINING AWARENESS OF SELF

Who are you? Answering that question is not so easy. A physiologist we know is fond of defining himself in terms of his own human anatomy and chemical composition. It is a very accurate description of who he is physiologically, but it leaves out all the other important, hard-to-define and intangible parts of our humanness that we call "self." What you take in with your senses (sight, hearing, touch, taste, smell), the interpretations (thoughts) in your head, your feelings (emotions), your intentions (wants, wishes, desires), and your own actions (behavior) are *you*, your *self*.

Your senses, thoughts, feelings, intentions, and actions are always part of you, but they are not always *within* your awareness.

Figure 2-1 The Awareness Wheel

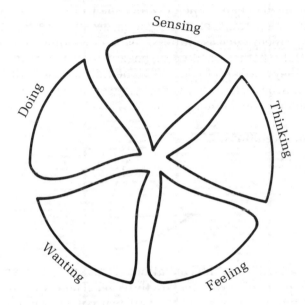

When we talk about "self-awareness," we're talking about awareness of these five dimensions. Increasing that awareness becomes a way of knowing yourself better; of becoming more conscious of who you are. And it can increase your choice about your self—to enjoy yourself as you are or to alter yourself—and increase your choice about whether or not to tell other people about yourself.

In this chapter, we want to help you experience more of your self, to help you become more aware of your many facets. No one has total self-awareness, not even for part of the time. Rather, self-awareness is a continuous process. To help you in this process, we are presenting a model—the Awareness Wheel. Keep in mind that the Awareness Wheel, like other models, is only a model. It is not "really" you. But many people have found it to be a very useful tool to help them to think about what is inside their selves. And using the Awareness Wheel may help you identify and clarify the different parts of your self.

These parts of you may be positive, such as when you are really feeling excited or happy and/or want to help others. Or they may be states we often think of as negative, because we don't like to perpetuate them, such as sadness, anger, or wanting to strike out at others. But whether positive or negative, all parts are valuable, because they are part of *you*. We hope this chapter will help you learn how to become more aware of yourself, and more appreciative of the unique person that you are.

Your Interpretations.

Let's start with your interpretations. That is the part many people are most aware of—what they're thinking. There are a number of kinds of interpretations, but they all share one thing in common: the thoughts you have about yourself, other people, things, and events. Some of the different kinds of interpretations also are called:

Impressions	Ideas
Beliefs	Opinions
Conclusions	Expectations
Assumptions	Stereotypes
Evaluations	Reasons

In short, interpretations are all the different kinds of *meanings* you make in your head to help you understand yourself, other people, and situations.

A key point to remember in understanding your interpretations is that they are constructed by you out of your past, present, and anticipated experiences. And because they are constructed, your interpretations probably will be somewhat different from another person's. Suppose a person was walking down the street, smiling.

People seeing this might interpret it in a number of different ways:

"He's excited because he just got a raise."

"He's enjoying the beautiful weather we're having."

"He's glad that the week is over and is thinking about his plans for the weekend."

"He's just found out that he got an 'A' on an exam."

The interpretations you make depend on the information your senses provide you and the thoughts you already have, as well as the immediate feelings, wants, and desires which you bring into the situation. For example, if I fail to see the smile (sense data) which accompanies my partner's "You nut!", I may conclude that I've just been put down (interpretation). This is more likely to happen if I don't see the smile and I'm already *feeling* depressed and disappointed. If I'm *feeling* pleased with myself, and both see the smile and hear the words, I may conclude that my partner is joking with me. If I *want* to have a serious discussion at that time, I may conclude (interpretation) that my partner is joking in order to avoid the discussion; but if I want to have a good time, I may conclude that my partner is joking and wants to have fun, too. So, "it all depends." The interpretations I make depend upon which sense data I take in, how I'm feeling, and what I want or desire. And we're not through yet!

Your interpretations are also influenced by the thoughts you *already* have in your head; that is, by your previous interpretations, especially by your *beliefs* (or assumptions). Returning to the example: if I believe that partners should not call each other names, even as a joke, then I may interpret my partner's remark as a putdown. But if I take for granted (assume) that partners can affectionately name-call now and then, I may take the remark to mean affection. Again, if I assumed—before the remark was made—my partner was mad at me, I'll interpret the comment different from the way I would interpret it if I assumed my partner was feeling affectionate toward me. Beliefs and assumptions can be powerful determinants of the interpretations we make.

Expectations are also prior interpretations which affect your immediate interpretations. For example, if my partner frequently jokes and sometimes affectionately name-calls as a joke, I learn to expect this and am more likely to interpret the remark as a joke. On the other hand, if I've never heard my partner call anyone a name except when angry then I don't expect my partner to joke in this way, and I'm not likely to conclude that s/he's very funny.

Your expectations grow out of your memory of past experiences and your intentions for the moment. If you've had mostly happy experiences with your supervisor in the past, and with other supervisors at other jobs, then if s/he calls you into the office for a talk, you probably will expect that something favorable is in the wind or at least that things will go well between you. But if you've had primarily unhappy experiences with superiors, even though you want things to go well this time, you may expect the worst.

It is important to achieve awareness of your own beliefs, expectations, and conclusions, just as it is important to be aware of your feelings, intentions, actions, and sense data. Sometimes your expectations and beliefs unwittingly lead to actions utterly incongruent with attaining your immediate goals. For example, Jim wanted to go bowling with Mary, but he expected her not to want to go, because he had noticed how tired she seemed. So he said, (in a tired, dubious tone), "You wouldn't want to go out bowling tonight, would you?" Mary replied, "No, not tonight." Later, Mary wondered why she had said no, because she really wanted to go bowling.

One of the most important points we want to make about interpretations is that *your interpretations are not simply based on the way things are, on some "reality out there."* They are based on what you perceive (sense) *plus* all the feelings, intentions, and prior interpretations you bring with you into each situation. Because of this, it's really not so surprising that two people can come to very different conclusions from the same sense data. "This couch is getting old and shabby looking," may mean to one listener that, "S/he is planning to go out shopping for a new one." The same remark passed between two different partners may mean "S/he's telling me I don't take good care of our furniture."

With this in mind, consider treating your interpretations (conclusions, impressions, evaluations, etc.) as tentative. This is useful for the following reasons:

1. It's hard to imagine a situation for which several interpretations are not possible from the same sensory data. Failure to see general alternative meanings leads to either/or, right/wrong type thinking.

2. Often, too little sense data is supplied in a situation in order to make a firm interpretation.

3. Many times the immediate sense data you receive is incomplete. Instead of trying to force a conclusion, keep your interpretation open to include all of the data.

4. Sometimes sense data conflicts with your prior experiences and present expectations. Again, forcing a conclusion causes you to ignore some important information.

5. Finally, sometimes you receive sense data with which you have had little or no experience. Making an interpretation too quickly here can preclude the possibility of seeing things in a new and different way.

We hope you will value your own ideas and your own interpretations (but keep them flexible!).

Your Sensations.

Sometimes those of us who believe we are "aware" persons find our awareness quite limited. There is so much we miss! But if we keep tuned into our senses, we can be more aware of what's going on around us.

Poets have great awareness of sensory data. Read how James Agee described a summer evening through the words of a small child: [1]

"On the rough wet grass of the back yard my father and mother have spread quilts. We all lie there, my mother, my father, my uncle, my aunt, and I too am lying there. First we were sitting up, then one of us lay down, and then we all lay down, on our stomachs, or on our sides, or on our backs, and they have kept on talking. They are not talking much, and talk is quiet, of nothing in particular, of nothing at all."

Your senses report raw data. They do the same kind of job that a good journalist does. That is, they observe and report and describe what you experience. But even good journalists' sense data often become confused with interpretations, and sometimes with feelings, too.

For example, a good reporter—using sense data only—might report something like this:

John Anthony walked slowly across campus. He was wearing blue jeans and an orange sweatshirt, and was carrying some books. He stopped to talk to a slender, dark-haired woman for a few minutes. After glancing at his watch, John and the woman then started briskly off toward the student union.

That's what an objective reporter could say based only on what he saw, with no interpretations. But watch what a different story it is if we mix in our own interpretation of the data.

John Anthony trudged wearily across campus. His steps were faltering, and he looked as though he didn't want to go to his next class. He stopped to talk with a pretty, dark-haired woman. It almost seemed as if he was looking for an excuse to cut class. They talked for a few minutes, then John glanced at his watch. Discovering that he was late for class anyway, John decided he wouldn't go. They drifted off to the student union for a cup of coffee.

[1]James Agee, A Death in the Family (New York: Bantam Books, 1969), p. 15.

These two different reports illustrate the difference between simply observing something and adding interpretations. Your senses are the source of all your data about the world. They are the funnel through which all information comes to you. But as you interpret what you see and hear, the data is filtered and transformed and added to. This simply happens. You can't really stop it from happening, and, in fact, you don't want to because we all need to make "sense" of what we see and hear. Being aware that sense data are different from other parts of the Awareness Wheel is very important. Yet this is one of the most difficult realizations for people. We'll talk more about why this is important in a moment, but first let's look at some more examples.

In one group, partners were asked to report what sense data they were observing about each other. They were instructed to omit interpretations, feelings, intentions, and so on, and stick only to descriptive sense data. The results:

"You look happy." (Happy is an interpretation. What sense data suggest the appearance of happiness? A smile, relaxed muscles, etc.)

"I see you making nervous movements with your foot." (Which of the senses says "nervous?" Nervous is an interpretation; the foot movements are the raw sense data.)

"I think you have lots of energy." (What's the data: posture, responsiveness, eyes, etc.?)

There is nothing wrong with making interpretations like these; in fact, as we pointed out, it's unavoidable. Further, these interpretations probably are accurate ones. So why is it important to be able to separate sense data from interpretations? *Because many times your interpretations are not accurate.* In the process of interpreting you make meaning out of what you see, hear, touch, etc. But if you remember that your interpretations are different from your observations, you're less likely to be caught in the trap of believing that what you think *is*—that your interpretation is *the* correct one. And further, you can increase your awareness by being able to go back to the raw sensory data to help yourself or other people see how you arrived at the interpretation you did.

Let's take some other examples. Sometimes our senses provide us with more information than we choose to use. Consider for a moment someone who uses only one sense, such as hearing. Things could develop like this:

> Ann and Bill are watching a basketball game. Ann snuggles up to Bill, smiles at him, and says, "I don't want to be here with you tonight." Bill, unfortunately, took in only the words. He replied, "Well, if you don't want to watch the game, why didn't you say so in the first place?"

Now, let's replay that, but this time, permit Bill to use *all* his senses:

> Ann and Bill are watching a basketball game. Ann snuggles up to Bill, smiles at him, and says, "I don't want to be here with you tonight." Bill feels her touch, catches her smile, smiles back and says softly, "I'd rather be someplace else with you, too."

This illustrates the way things can turn out differently when we use all of our sense data instead of just a part of it. But sometimes we receive multiple data that conflict. Here's an example:

> Fred asked Denise to go to the movies with him. She replied, "I'd love to go," in a flat, tired tone of voice. (The words convey "I want to," but the tone conveys "I don't want to.")

Multiple data, where one part is in disagreement with another, are commonplace in everyday human interaction. When this happens, we find it useful to comment on the discrepancy.

> Fred replied, "I don't know what to believe. Your voice sounds tired to me, but your words say you're interested in going."

We have illustrated two common problems people have in using sense data. One is that they don't pay enough attention to the data reaching their various senses, and the second is that they receive conflicting data. A third problem, described previously, is that people sometimes jump to conclusions too hastily without being aware of their sense data. If you are aware that your interpretations and your sense data are not one and the same, you'll be able to test and clarify and alter your interpretations when it's important by moving back and forth between the sense data and your interpretations.

Your Feelings.

Slippery, elusive, wonderful, or horrible; your feelings are your spontaneous *responses* to the interpretations you make and the expectations you have. These emotional responses are inside your body, though they may have outward signs. For example, when you feel angry inside, your outward signs may be tense muscles, flushed skin, loud, rapid speech, etc. Or when you feel sad inside, the outside sign may be tears. When you feel elated inside, you may smile, laugh, or joke. To help you identify some typical feelings or emotions, here is a partial list of feelings that people experience:

pleased	confused	eager	uncomfortable
comfortable	excited	weary	discontented
calm	lonely	angry	anxious
satisfied	elated	glad	solemn
bored	uneasy	grief	apathetic
jubilant	silly	contented	hopeful
fearful	hesitant	cautious	sad
daring	surprised	confident	proud

Feelings are important in their own right. Your feelings are you, the person you are. But they're also important because they serve several functions.

First, they may serve as a *barometer. Feelings can alert you to "what's going on" and help you to understand your reaction to a situation.*

> Tom was listening to Alice explain why she couldn't spend the weekend with him. Her reasons were very rational and logical. Tom liked to think of himself as an accepting, understanding fellow. But as he paid attention to his barometer he felt his face become hot and his heart began to beat more rapidly. He knew he was angry and disappointed.

> Silently, as Tom thought about the situation he began shutting Alice out, withdrawing. As he did this he became aware of feeling sad. At first he tried to ignore his sadness, but then he acknowledged it, realizing that Alice was very important to him and that it was painful for him to hurt her intentionally.

A second function of your feelings is to help you clarify your expectations. Some of your feelings are felt because of a difference between what you *expect* and what you actually *experience*. If, for example, you expect to be accepted by another person, but find instead that you are rejected, you'll probably feel surprised, crushed, or infuriated. On the other hand, if you expect to be rejected and instead find yourself accepted, you'll probably feel happy, excited, or gratified. As you see, these discrepancies in expectations result in either positive or negative feelings.

Another kind of discrepancy can occur when you really don't have any expectation, but something happens, anyway. These can lead to either negative or positive feelings, too. For example, if you are not planning to do anything during the evening, but a friend calls up and wants to get together, you are likely to have good feelings. However, if some one calls unexpectedly to tell you that a relative is sick, negative feelings occur.

In these examples, you understand your expectations in the situation. However, in many situations, people aren't really clear about what they expect to happen. That is when feelings can be helpful in clarifying expectations. Work out these examples to see how feelings can clarify your expectations.

> Suppose you ask your partner to do something that will take a lot of time and energy. Your partner says, "I'll be glad to do it," and you feel elated. What expectations did you have about your partner's response?

> You prepare a very special dinner for your partner, but your partner only picks at his/her food. You feel disappointed, let down. What expectations did you have?

> You receive an 'A' on a final exam and experience a feeling of amazement and elation. What had been your expectation?

In short, feelings can serve either the function of helping you to better understand a situation or of clarifying your expectations in a situation. But feelings can only serve these functions if you let yourself be aware of them.

If you allow yourself to experience your feelings rather than repress or deny them, they can be useful to you. Most people, when the talk turns to avoiding feelings, think first of denying negative feelings. But sometimes positive feelings are denied, too. Why? Because it's often uncomfortable to acknowledge and experience how important your partner may be to you; the good feelings that come from being with him or her, and how much you care.

In order to bring feeling into your awareness, there are a number of signals to watch for. First, there are physiological signs, such as sweating, rapid heartbeat, a feeling of lightness, and all the other bodily signs that accompany feelings. Then there are behavioral signs, things you do to demonstrate what you're feeling. When you avoid eye contact, get quiet, laugh, or make love, you're expressing your feelings through a behavioral sign. There are more indirect signs, such as when you feel appreciation and instead of expressing that directly, you buy your partner a gift. Or you may tell your partner how stupid s/he is when you're feeling angry. That is indirect expression.

Feelings can't be controlled by ignoring them or done away with by denying them. But they may change as you permit yourself to reassess sense data and the interpretations you've made. In short, reconstructing expectations and interpretations (reframing or redefining the situation) can give rise to new and different feelings.

> Barb was mad at Mike because he didn't want to go out Friday night to celebrate her promotion. He said he'd rather wait till Saturday. Barb felt disappointed and upset because it seemed to her that her promotion didn't merit immediate celebration in Mike's eyes. Then she recalled how exhausted he looked, and remembered that it must have been 100° in the greenhouse where he worked. She concluded that his wishing to postpone had nothing to do with his valuing her promotion, but was simply "where he was at," that is, dead tired. Barb still felt disappointed, but was no longer upset with Mike.

At other times, it's useful just "to go with" what you feel. Regardless of what you're feeling, feel it more—really experience it—let it happen. If you're sad, let your sadness amplify; don't fight it by trying to alter it. Likewise, if you're delighted, take it higher; don't hold back. Feelings have their own natural course if we allow them to ebb and flow with where we are. In fact, it's almost impossible to keep them from changing if you permit yourself to be uniquely you.

As we said, there is no such thing as controlling feelings by ignoring them or denying them. Rather, when you attempt to deny or ignore your feelings, you give up control of them and allow them to control you. It's natural for you to have feelings. We hope that you learn to accept them as yours. Feelings don't have to be justified, explained, or apologized for. You are human, so you feel. As you become more in tune with your feelings, you'll learn to recognize what they're telling you about yourself and the situation.

Feelings can be identified and they can be very useful for you. But we may have made it sound easier than it really is. One of the difficult things about feelings is that very often you "feel" in combinations. When you feel a single feeling, it's usually a lot easier to identify. You may, for example, feel irritated. But you may feel irritated and cautious in combination. And you may feel irritated, cautious, and contentious all at the same time. So, when someone asks you "what are you feeling?" it's harder to sort out and say exactly what you are feeling. To complicate matters further, the intensity of feelings varies. That is, you may be *very* relaxed, *fairly* relaxed, *mildly* relaxed, and sometimes *almost* relaxed.

Finally, your multiple feelings can be in conflict. When they are, you're very likely to give conflicting information when you express your feelings.

> A friend was waiting for his wife one evening, and as it got later and later, he began to construct a series of interpretations and experience a variety of feelings:
>
> Concern (that she may have had an accident)
>
> Anger (that she may have forgotten he was waiting)
>
> Regret (that he had not been clearer about where to meet each other).
>
> When she arrived, she asked, "Are you upset with me?" He replied, "Upset? I'm mad! But I'm happy to see you too, because I was worried that you might have had an accident. I don't like to wait."

So, even though feelings can be complicated, and even in conflict, if you are able to identify them, you can express them. We'll talk more about expression of feelings in the next chapter.

Your Intentions.

"Intention" has a broad meaning. It is usually taken to mean a general attitude of moving toward or away from something.

Because it has a broad meaning, intention can be used to signify anything from your immediate desire in a situation to what you'd like to accomplish during the day, to long-range goals for several years or a lifetime. For present purposes, we would like you to think of intentions as your immediate desires; things you want or don't want for yourself in a specific situation. These shorter term intentions are the ones most people have difficulty being aware of.

Actually, intentions are quite difficult to identify because they can easily be mixed up with what you would like others to do. When this happens, your intentions for others often come out in the form of questions or commands. The "I want" is unspoken. For example, frequently people say to others:

> "You should finish the job as soon as possible," rather than "I'd like you to . . . "

> "Would you like to go to the movie with me," rather than, "I'd like to go to a movie with you."

> "You shouldn't do that," rather than, "I want you to stop doing that."

What they are often expressing in a very indirect way is their intention—what they want for themselves in the situation.

As you might imagine, people have many different kinds of intentions. Here is a list to help you recognize the kinds of intentions people often have:

to approach	to praise	to conceal
to reject	to defend self	to play
to support	to hurt	to explore
to persuade	to be friendly	to be caring
to be funny	to ponder	to listen
to ignore	to help	to disregard
to clarify	to accept	to share
to avoid	to demand	to understand
to cooperate	to be honest	to be responsive

Quite often, intentions are a kind of "hidden agenda" inside yourself. Intentions become hidden agenda because (1) you are unaware of all of your intentions at times, or (2) you are aware of them, but you simply forget or think they're not important enough to disclose to another, or (3) you choose to keep your intentions hidden from others on purpose. For example, an intention you might choose *not* to disclose could be one of the following:

"I want to get even with you."

"I want you to admire me."

"I want to help you feel good about yourself."

In general, we believe that people don't disclose their intentions to others frequently enough. Sometimes this happens because they are not aware of their intention, but more often because they don't treat their intentions as important. This is unfortunate because intentions have a very significant function.

Intentions are powerful because they have such a big impact on your actions. Changes in your actions often really require changes in your intentions. While you can "fake" your own behavior to a certain extent, it's hard to fake your intentions—what's inside you. You only fool yourself when you do this. Only *you* can really know your intentions because your intentions are within you and inaccessible to others. So in an important sense, honesty to yourself is intimately connected to your intentions.

Think of your intentions as "organizers." Probably the most important function of intentions is to help you consider alternative actions, things you *want* and *don't want* to do. For example, suppose you want your partner to be pleased with you. Identifying that intention can help you to identify possible actions to support your intentions:

Listen carefully to your partner.

Do something nice, such as buy a gift or arrange something special for the two of you.

Offer to do some chore that your partner usually does.

We know that this sounds awfully "rational," probably more so than you feel comfortable with. And in a way it is. We don't really think people can or should try to analyze their intentions all the time. But we do think that when something important is happening between you and your partner, or when you are feeling quite dissatisfied, identifying *what you want*—your intention—can be very helpful in clarifying for yourself what is happening.

Sometimes it's not easy to maintain awareness of your own intentions. One thing you can do to help identify your intentions is swing to the "action" dimension of your Awareness Wheel and look at your own behavior. Believe your behavior! If you do something, it's likely that you wanted to do it, or, at least there was something you wanted for yourself that that action appeared likely to (You may have had other wants at the same time which were not achieved by what you did, but we'll talk about mixed and contradictory intentions a little later). Don't deny your behavior; most of the time your behavior provides good clues to your intentions.

Feelings also can tell you about your intentions. Positive feelings, feeling satisfied, feeling "okay" usually means that your major intentions match your behavior. When you don't feel satisfied; when you feel irritable or unhappy, it can mean that your more important intentions are not matching your behavior.

A third way to identify your intentions is to think about some of the things you admit to yourself privately but are unwilling to admit to others. As we noted above, it's hard to fake your intentions because when you do this, you're trying to kid yourself. And most people don't like to do this. So look for the things you will admit only to yourself; they can provide significant clues to what you want for yourself in a situation.

Intentions, like feelings, can be held singly. But just as with feelings, intentions are held in combinations more often. And also like feelings, intentions vary in their intensity.

"I want to hear and understand you, and I want you to hear and understand me."

"I want us to have a good time. I want you to like me. I want us to become closer."

"I kind of want to have fun tonight, but most of all I'd just like to relax."

As we saw with feelings, sometimes the combination of intentions may be in conflict. Conflicting intentions can result in confusing behavior unless you're aware of them.

"Part of me wants to be with you, and part of me wants to be by myself right now."

"I want to strike out at you because I'm angry, but I don't want to put a barrier between us, either."

Each of these examples illustrates a conflict between immediate intentions. People also commonly experience conflicts between immediate and longer range intentions.

"I want to do well on my exam tomorrow, but I want to be with you now, too."

"I want us to have an attractive house that we can be proud of, but I want to relax today and not go furniture shopping."

And, of course, we also frequently experience tensions between several longer range intentions.

"I want to do something different and see new places on our vacation, but I also don't want to waste a lot of time driving."

"I want to get good grades, but I don't want to spend all my time studying."

All of these examples show that conflicting intentions, like conflicting feelings, can be expressed if you are able to identify them. We'll talk more about expressing intentions in the next chapter. Now let's move on to the last spoke in the Awareness Wheel.

Your Actions.

Most of us like to believe that we "know what we're doing." We assume we're aware of what we're doing or have done, but frequently some of our actions are not part of our awareness. We're often not aware of a number of important behaviors that others observe. One part of your behavior of which your partner probably is more aware than you are, is the punctuation of your conversation. These are your interruptions, pauses, incomplete sentences, etc. For example, many smokers reach for a cigarette as a way of punctuating, interrupting, or delaying a conversation that has become tense. Or you may not be aware of your own level of attention in a prior situation. You may not know how closely you have been listening—or not listening—to your partner. Bodily posture, facial expressions, and voice characteristics are actions your partner may have tuned into, but of which you may have little awareness.

It's hard to be aware of all of your actions because so much is happening at one time. But your actions become sense data from which your partner makes interpretations.

> Ray and Bev were listening to some of Bev's record albums. She turned to him and asked, "Do you like this one?"
>
> Ray hesitated and after a pause said, "Yeah, I like it."
>
> Bev said, "Your voice doesn't sound as if you like it."

Ray stood up and walked around the room looking at some of Bev's plants. Then he said, "I guess I really do like it."

Ray is not aware of all his actions, but his actions are supplying Bev with quite a bit of data from which she is drawing her conclusion.

There's a problem in maintaining awareness of actions. If you're constantly aware of your actions, you're not likely to be spontaneous. Continually monitoring your actions will probably take a lot of fun out of your activities and your relationships. But actions are important to you for self-information. And it can be useful for you to take a look at some of your patterns; being aware of the behavior and actions which you *repeat* in particular kinds of situations will help you change them if you want to, or at least let you know what message you're giving your partner. One of the authors, for example, drops his voice to a near whisper at the end of a sentence, when he's not confident about what he's saying. Another removes his glasses when he's called upon to answer a question about which he's not certain.

Taking a look at some of your actions as they occur, or have occurred in the past, will also help you understand the impact you're having on your partner. Ray's actions communicated to Bev more than his words did. Remember, your actions are a part of you and become the raw data that your partner's senses take in. Being aware of your actions is not an easy matter, and not something to monitor all the time. But knowing what you are doing can be an immense help to you.

PUTTING THE AWARENESS WHEEL TOGETHER AND LEARNING HOW TO USE IT

One way of using the Awareness Wheel is to work your way around it, step-by-step:

"I see you sitting there reading quietly (sensing), and I think you must be relaxed and contented (interpreting). I feel very happy (feeling), and I want to leave you alone so you can enjoy yourself (intending). So I leave you alone (action).

Moving through the Awareness Wheel in a sequential, step-by-step fashion can be done, but there are other ways to use it, too. In fact, awareness in every-day life probably happens more often in other ways, frequently beginning with feelings.

"I'm excited today" (feeling); grabs partner and swings around playfully (action). "It must be because I'm looking forward to having you to myself all day" (interpretation). "When I see your eyes sparkle like this (sensation), I think you're beautiful (interpretation). I really want to be with you today (intention)."

Tune into your Awareness Wheel right now. Go with your awareness. What comes to you first? Your feelings? Your intentions? Your thoughts? Your senses? Your actions? Most people are more in touch with one dimension of the Awareness Wheel than others. When they begin to tune in on their own awareness, one dimension seems regularly to come first.

Betty usually experienced her feeling dimension first. "I love it here; it feels so free." From that dimension she usually moved to intentions. " I want to just stand here and enjoy it all." And then she would usually tune into her interpretations. "I think this is a wonderful place." And finally she would let herself in on the sense data. "The trees are green, the birds active, and the lake is so blue."

Charlie, on the other hand, was a "sensation" man. "Man, look at all the people here today (senses). I'm uncomfortable (feelings). This place is too crowded for me (interpretation). I'm getting out of here (intention)." He leaves (action).

George usually became aware of his intentions first. "I want to get away from you (intention). When you're as mad as you are (interpretation), I feel anxious (feeling). The way you're yelling and stamping around (senses)!"

What's your pattern? Can you identify it? How about your partner's pattern? How does it differ from yours? Very few partners have the same pattern. Having different patterns adds variety to the relationship, but it can create difficulties if you are unaware that your partner experiences a situation very differently from you, or if you believe that partners should always see things the same way. If you know something about your own pattern, and know and accept your partner's pattern, you've already enhanced your understanding of each other.

Why Use the Awareness Wheel?

Putting your Awareness Wheel together really is a second kind of interpretation. In our earlier discussion of interpretations, we put the greatest emphasis on the meanings you make from the sense data you receive. We did this because we were focusing on the kinds of interpretations you make about people and events in the world outside yourself—your senses keep you in touch with these things. But your interpretations about yourself don't rely only on data gathered by your senses. Rather, these interpretations depend to a much greater extent on information you have inside yourself, especially your feelings and intentions. So in a very real way, when you use your Awareness Wheel, you are increasing the information available to you for understanding and interpreting yourself.

The Awareness Wheel can help you to *know yourself* more effectively, moment by moment, if you wish. There are many parts to you—many different dimensions contribute to you; the whole person. Keeping in mind the various spokes of your Awareness Wheel can help you better identify and clarify these various dimensions. Use of the Awareness Wheel can eliminate confusion and help you to better understand your experience. It can help you think through situations by generating more information about yourself. The Awareness Wheel can also help you become a more integrated person, help you clarify and understand how the many dimensions of your self are related. In short, using your Awareness Wheel can get you more in touch with yourself at a given moment and thus help you learn more about yourself.

Increasing your understanding of yourself through using your Awareness Wheel has a second major benefit. It increases your *choices*. The information in the wheel becomes a basis for making choices regarding yourself and what you want to do. The Awareness Wheel helps give you a better idea of where you're coming from; what you take in, what you think, what you feel, and what you want. When you know where you're coming from, the choices you make are much more likely to be self-fulfilling and satisfying. When you neglect self-information and operate from limited awareness, you're likely to find yourself in misunderstandings, conflicts, and taking less effective action.

A third reason for using the Awareness Wheel for increasing self-awareness involves your relationships with your partner and other people. You can choose to communicate verbally to your partner only information of which you are aware. Increasing your information about yourself expands the range of possibilities of what you can communicate. And because the Awareness Wheel helps you identify more information, it can help your communication with your partner become more complete—if you want it to be. *Your intentional communication is limited by the degree of your self-awareness.* Using the Awareness Wheel can enlarge your range of choices about what to communicate, and can help you be more open to your partner if that's what you want.

In the next two chapters, we'll talk some more about self-awareness. The following chapter shows you how to disclose information from your own Awareness Wheel. In the chapter after that, we'll look at different types of limited awareness and discuss the impacts they have on you and your partner.

But before moving on, we'd like to mention a final reason for increasing your self-awareness. Increased self-awareness may lead to increased self-esteem and self-confidence. When you have a clear picture of your thoughts, feelings, intentions, and actions, you're very likely to become aware of your own uniqueness. You are the authority on your own awareness, and your own unique awareness is very valuable. Nobody else in the world is exactly like you. At any moment, you are the only person in the world, sensing, thinking, wanting and doing *exactly* as you are. Your uniqueness has a value all of its own. These precise dimensions, at this moment, won't be duplicated by you or anyone else in the future. Talk about the value of rare stamps or gems! What about the rarest of all?—You! Only one of you exists and that makes you priceless.

So, go with your experience, increase your awareness, and accept, affirm, and make use of it.

CHAPTER THREE

DISCLOSING SELF AWARENESS

SELF-DISCLOSURE SKILLS

Now that you can identify the parts that go into your own awareness, let's consider the ways in which you can let other people know what's going on inside of you.

> Ellen and Ted were sitting in a quiet corner of the restaurant. Ted was tapping his fingers on the table, while Ellen kept her eyes focused on her plate. She was rubbing a chip on the plate with her finger. She said, "Ted, this is difficult for me to say, but I don't want to play cat and mouse with you and it's important to me that you know my situation. When we're together and joke and tease, I feel warm and good all over. But sometimes I think you're getting more serious than I want to get. Like last night. You started saying some things about the future that just don't fit with what I want from our relationship now. Right now, when I hear myself saying these things, I begin to get uncomfortable, because I want to be with you, but I don't want to get too serious, and I'm afraid you'll get angry and not want to see me again."

Ellen has done an excellent job of disclosing what was going on inside of herself by making process statements to Ted. Six skills are illustrated in her messages: speaking for self, making sense statements, making interpretive statements, making feeling statements, making intention statements, and making action statements. Let's examine each of these.

Skill #1: Speaking for Self.

The first skill, speaking for self, is prerequisite to all other skills. When you speak for yourself, you *identify* yourself as being central in your awareness, and you're very clear about this in your communication. You are the person who's alive to and aware of your own experience. You report your own sensations, your own thoughts, your own feelings, your own intentions, and your own actions—and you clearly indicate that, indeed, you are the owner. The phrases: "I think . . ." "I feel . . ." "I want . . ." identify you as the source of your awareness. But "speaking for self" also means that you are not the expert on your partner's inner experience. You own *your* Awareness Wheel, and you are responsible for it, but you don't own your partner's Awareness Wheel, and you can't be responsible for it. If you try to speak for your partner and say what he or she thinks, feels, or wants, you are, in effect, claiming ownership and responsibility for your partner's Awareness Wheel.

When you speak for self, you use "I," "me," "my," and "mine." But that's terrible isn't it? Aren't people who frequently refer to themselves self-centered and selfish? This notion grows out of early experiences, where many of us were taught to avoid referring to ourself. We were told that to do so means you think too much of yourself. (One of the authors remembers learning how to write a letter to a friend without using the word "I!") We assume you are reading this book to become a better communicator about yourself. And communicating clearly about yourself without using personal pronouns—the source of your awareness—is impossible. Notice how the statements below identify the speaker. There is no question about whose experience it is.

"It's important to me."

"I want more time to think about it."

"My impression is different."

"I'll get the assignment completed by Thursday."

"I'm really pleased about your progress."

"I saw the most beautiful sunset I've ever seen. The sky was completely full of a glowing, orange light. I wanted to stop it from fading."

These statements indicate that the speaker recognizes his feelings, intentions, and actions. He's the authority on his own awareness.

Oddly enough, our teachers were right—heavy use of "I," "me," "my," and "mine" does, indeed, indicate that you think highly of yourself. What is odd to us is that this was once thought to be undesirable! We *want* to value ourselves, and we hope you will value yourselves and convey this in your communication. Speaking for self indicates self-valuing.

Valuing of self and valuing of partner seem to be closely connected. We think it's pretty difficult to value one's partner without valuing oneself. Furthermore, you may subtly discourage your partner from valuing you unless you clearly communicate that you value yourself. If you don't speak for yourself, you may be sending confusing messages.

"There's a good movie showing at the World this week."

"Most people would be mad if this happened to them, don't you think?"

"It might be good for us to be more open with each other."

These are examples of what we call *under-responsible* statements. A characteristic of under-responsible statements is that they speak for *no one*; rather they substitute "it," "some people," or "one" for "I". Or, they include no pronoun or reference at all. As a result, the ownership of the statement is left in question. The opinions, intentions, or feelings of the under-responsible speaker can only be guessed at, because they're voiced in such a cautious, uncommitted way. The speaker doesn't appear to value them enough to claim them directly. In time, if he continually talks in an under-responsible way, he may succeed in getting others to devalue his opinions, intentions, and feelings, because he fails to acknowledge and own his own experience.

Another way to avoid speaking for self is by speaking for others, *over-responsibility*. Over-responsible statements sound like this:

"What movie should we go to? You'd like the one at the World. It's just the kind you like."

"You don't understand at all why I'm mad!"

"We should be more open."

"All men feel that way."

A characteristic of over-responsible statements is that they speak for *others* by substituting "you," "we," "everybody," or "all" for "I," frequently coupled with "should" and "oughts." When you communicate in an over-responsible manner, you assert that you know better than the other person what is going on inside of him or what he should do. If you frequently speak for your partner, s/he may experience an uneasy feeling of being hemmed in, trapped; a feeling of having too little room to be himself. Under-responsible communication and over-responsible communication are alike in one respect: in failing to disclose directly what the speaker thinks, feels, or wants.

The *self-responsible* person speaks for self. He recognizes his own awareness and identifies his experiences as his own. Simultaneously, he leaves room for others to see and to experience things differently by letting them speak for themselves. In fact, self-responsible communication encourages disclosure of differences. In contrast, under-responsible communication tends to conceal differences and over-responsbile communication tends to coerce agreement. To sum up, acting self-responsibly by speaking for self:

—demonstrates that you are central in your awareness.

—clearly identifies yourself as the source of the messages you send.

—says that you are the owner of your perceptions, thoughts, feelings, wants, and actions.

—shows regard for yourself.

—leaves room for your partner to be self-responsible, too.

—adds to the accuracy and quality of your communication.

When you take full charge of yourself, acknowledging, disclosing, and accepting responsibility for your own Awareness Wheel, suddenly your partner has all kinds of room to do the same for him/herself. It's neat when this happens! The "blame game" can stop. There are no more conflicts about who's responsible for whom. You both know—each is responsible for his/her own self. Listen to this:

> Judy: "When you first started to let me know directly what you thought or how you felt, it took some getting used to. I wanted you to, but it was kind of a jolt at times."
>
> Mike: "Yeah. I remember sometimes when you seemed really surprised when I tuned in to myself and let you know what was going on inside me. Sometimes I surprised myself, too."
>
> Judy: "It wasn't only that you were more aware of yourself. You began refusing to be responsible for me, too, and that really changed things."
>
> Mike: "I think that's right."

Skill #2: Making Sense Statements.

Making sense statements is the skill of describing *what you see, hear, touch, taste, and smell*. It's the skill of reporting on the sense data you receive. Sense statements are used in the process of *documenting*. By "documenting," we mean the process of describing what you see, hear, etc. that leads you to your interpretation.

> *Bill:* "I think you're preoccupied with something tonight." (here, Bill is stating his interpretation without describing the data.)
>
> *Joan:* "Really? What makes you say that?" (Joan is asking him to describe and report the data.)
>
> *Bill:* "I see you staring into space and not answering me. I think your mind must be somewhere else." (Bill documents his conclusion with a specific sense statement and rephrases his interpretation.)

The essence of making a sense statement is *being specific*, that is, being specific about time, location, and action or behavior. The more specific the sense statement, the more useful it usually is. It is useful because it helps your partner find your point of reference, and avoids labeling or making global judgments about your partner when you are referring to his actions.

Sample documenting statements:

> "Yesterday, when you first got up . . . (specific about time)
>
> "I was at the park today and saw . . . (specific about place)
>
> "Just as you began to respond to my question I saw you pause, look down, and then I heard you say . . . (specific about other's actions)

In short, sense statements help your partner orient himself to your experiences. And in a very real way they are an aid to you in "making sense" out of your *own* experience. Sense statements provide descriptions of situations from the past, report observations about the present moment, or anticipate future cues. In doing so, they supply data to "what," "where," "when," "how," and "who" types of questions. (They don't explain "why," however. Why takes you to reasons and interpretations, not to more data!)

Documenting with sense statements (descriptive, sensory data) is important for several reasons:

1. It increases your understanding of yourself. It gives you a better idea of how you arrived at your own interpretations, and a better idea of what your feelings and intentions are related to.

2. It gives your partner a much clearer idea of what specifically it is you are referring to, and provides a chance for your partner to clarify his message if it's been understood. It puts the data you're operating from "on the table." This gives your partner a chance to tell you how he's responding to the same data, as in the following example:

> *John:* "I don't think you like my new suit."
>
> *Carol:* "That's not true! What makes you say that?"
>
> *John:* (documenting) "When I tried it on for you, you were very quiet and you were grinning."
>
> *Carol:* "Wait a second. I was quiet because I was thinking about how nice you looked. I guess I was grinning because I'm proud of you."

3. Documenting makes a "yes, I am/no, I'm not" argument harder to start and more difficult to continue. It makes clear that you're talking about your own perceptions and interpretations, not about some absolute and irrefutable "truth."

4. It helps avoid the pitfall of making global judgments about your partner's personality or character. Contrast the following statements:

> "I get frustrated that you're such a careless money-manager." (global evaluation)
>
> "I got frustrated last night when I saw you hadn't recorded the checks you'd written." (documenting)

5. Documenting with descriptive sense data is a way of valuing your partner. It takes effort to document, to provide more information for your partner.

Let's look at an example to see how documenting can be helpful. One couple decided that they would go out for dinner:

Jim: "We haven't had French cuisine for a long time. How about going out to Le Chateau?"

Kate: (wrinkling her nose) "Well . . . I think that would be okay."

Jim: "It looks to me like that's not exactly your first choice. When you wrinkle your nose and answer kind of slow, I get the impression you'd just as soon go some place else."

Kate: (pausing) "Well, I know you like French food a lot, and so do I usually. But tonight I'd rather go some place that has music and dancing along with dinner. How about the Edgewater Inn instead?"

Hearing her partner's observations, Kate was able to clarify her message without getting into an argument about Jim's interpretation. Be careful though: It's a *misuse* of documenting to try to prove *a point* with data; to try to force your partner to see it your way. How do you think Kate would have responded if Jim had documented his interpretation like this?

Jim: "When you wrinkle up your nose and answer kind of slow, that's a sure sign you don't want to do something. Don't try to deny it. It's okay with me if we go someplace else."

Jim leaves little room for Kate to tune in to herself and clarify for herself and for Jim what she wants most at this point. Kate is likely to feel pushed into either "admitting" he's right or denying it. Documenting is helpful in communication when it is used to clarify and provide information, not when it is used to prove or to justify a point.

Try not to use the word "when" by itself for documentation. By itself, "when" is generally not specific enough in time or place.

Compare:

"When I think you aren't interested in what I'm saying I feel
. . . "

with,

"Last night, after supper, when we sat down together a few moments and began sharing some of our experiences of the day, I thought you weren't interested in what I was saying. I felt
. . . "

Specific descriptive data is often more useful in helping your partner tune into your particular concern than is provided just by the word "when." Specific data helps your partner tune into your exact meaning. In the illustration above, it will also be important for the speaker to describe exactly the behavior s/he is referring to that led to the conclusion "not interested."

Before ending this section, we want to emphasize again the usefulness of making sense statements when it's your intention to provide "feedback" to your partner, either to request a change in what your partner is doing or to confirm and reinforce something you like. The descriptive data provides a basis for creating understanding. It helps your partner to understand specifically what you want.

For example, take the statement, "I got frustrated last night when I saw you hadn't recorded the checks you'd written in the check book because I'm afraid I might overdraw the account." Very specific information has been provided, information about the other's behavior and the impact of this behavior on self. However, a statement like "I don't think you know how to handle money," communicates some displeasure and a wish for the other to change, but leaves the other to guess what it's all about. Does s/he mean you don't consult him/her enough? Does s/he mean you spend too much on food? On clothes? Or is s/he just trying to make you feel bad?

To summarize briefly, documenting can be extremely useful in helping to increase self-awareness and understanding between partners. It is sometimes misused to prove or to justify. Documenting with sense statements is likely to be particularly useful when you and your partner are considering change in your actions.

Skill #3: Making Interpretive Statements.

Some people are surprised to discover that making an interpretive statement is a skill worth paying attention to. Here are some of the reasons for the surprise. People think:

—Interpretations are so common, everyone knows how to say what they think, so why pay any particular attention to it.
—Interpretations are bad—they stereotype, evaluate and categorize people and things.
—Saying what you think means you're operating "in your head" and "gut" feelings are what really count.

Our experience leads us to believe that making clear interpretive statements is a skill. Since interpretations are common, they can be easily and sloppily made, confusing communication. In addition, it's normal to think in categories and this is particularly useful when you realize what you are doing, when you own your interpretations, and include room for others to see things differently. Finally, while your feelings are important, so are your thoughts. We don't think one can be sacrificed for the other—they're two different and important types of awareness.

Our intention, then, for encouraging you to view disclosing your thoughts as a skill is to help you see that the making of meaning (interpretations) is an ongoing process—something you're creating, perpetuating, modifying, or destroying over time. You are constantly making your own meaning in every situation.

What is important is that you recognize your own interpretations as a unique dimension of your Awareness Wheel and treat them as flexible hypotheses for organizing your current thinking. If you recognize this and disclose them to your partner by speaking for yourself, you are saying:

—This is my thinking at this point in time and is subject to change with new data.

—I'm examining and testing my interpretations with my own experience (awareness). They are situation-bound and not true for all time.

—I'm appreciating my own uniqueness rather than my rightness or wrongness.

—I am in charge of my own meanings—I can see and propose alternative meanings, too.

—Finally, my interpretation of a situation is not the way the world *is;* its the way I am organizing what I see and hear at this point in time. I expect you to see many things differently.

Interpreting statements can be made simply by saying *what* it is you're thinking, believing, assuming, etc. They need not be vague, general, illusive; rather, they can be clear, concise, and focused if you experience them this way. Be careful, though, to speak about your own awareness—to identify your thoughts as being your own. If you don't, others may think you're speaking for them and this can create troubled communication.

Here are some examples of interpreting statements:

"I think it's time to stop."

"It's my impression you'd be interested in going."

"It seems possible to me."

"I think it's the wrong way to go about it."

"I think you've got my point."

"I'm wondering if you're feeling what I'm feeling."

"I expect to be on time."

"The reason I'm calling is to see if you'd like to get together tonight."

Notice, all these statements are undocumented interpretations. In a conversation, some of them might require some documentation with sense statements to help your partner see how you arrived at your interpretation.

Skill #4. Making Feeling Statements.

In order to make feeling statements, it's important to begin by recognizing that the feeling is yours—that it belongs to you. Recognizing your own feelings is the first step. It's not always easy to say to yourself, "I feel envious, greedy, or jealous," to name a few feelings that people frequently disown. And for many people, it's just as difficult to acknowledge positive feelings like caring, affection, and joy. But as human beings, we do have these feelings.

Feelings are commonly expressed through non-verbal behavior, either indirectly and symbolically (buying a gift; staying away) or directly (kissing; laughing; crying; slamming doors; storming around). Non-verbal expressions of feelings often have high impact. In some situations actions *do* "speak louder than words," demonstrating that something is going on inside of you, that you have feelings. For this reason, people often assume that these kinds of behaviors are "clear" expressions of feelings. But this isn't always the case. Take crying, for example. Do the tears express sadness, disappointment, anger, joy, or relief? Does the gift mean affection or guilt? "Can't s/he tell how I feel by the way I act?" The answer to this question is "maybe not." The fact is, non-verbal behavior may be convincing (actions speak louder. . .), but *words* may be needed to clarify exactly what it is you are feeling. If you've ever been around a mother with a crying infant who could not be comforted you must have heard, "I just wish he could *talk* and tell me what's the matter!" When you want to let your partner know directly and clearly what you're feeling, make feeling statements.

You can verbalize your feelings directly and clearly . by describing specifically the feelings you have. You simply say, "I feel . . .," or "I'm . . . " as in the following examples:

"I'm really happy about the way the project is working out!"

"I'm feeling anxious about that exam."

"I'm surprised."

"I sure feel relieved, hearing that from you!"

"Right now, I'm feeling contented and happy and relaxed."

"I'm really disappointed, and mad, too!"

Even mixed feeling can be expressed directly. All you have to do is identify and disclose the various feelings you are having.

Ron: "How would you like to take a couple weeks vacation?"

Pat: "I'd love to. It sounds exciting but I'm also worried about whether we can afford it. Do you really think we can?"

So if this is all you have to do, you might well ask, why do we call making feeling statements a *skill?* That's a fair question. We'd like to answer it by pointing to some of the difficulties you may experience in making feeling statements.

First, there are difficulties in being aware of the feelings you experience and acknowledging to yourself what the feelings are. Perhaps this is the hardest part: identifying the feelings you have inside of yourself.

Second, you may experience discomfort in verbally disclosing your feelings directly, because our culture places a high priority on the control of emotions. "Men don't cry." "Women don't raise their voices, or slam doors, or swear." Most of us have been brought up to keep feelings behind a closed door marked "Private."

Third, disclosing feelings often seems risky. When you tell someone directly what you are feeling, you make yourself vulnerable—vulnerable to rejection, to being seen as silly, weak, unusual, or to many other kinds of negative evaluations. And disclosing positive feelings can be experienced as even more risky, perhaps because you're committing yourself to something or someone:

> *Mary:* "I really care a lot for you, Bob."
>
> *Bob:* (moving away slightly): "I like you, too, Mary."

"Shall I disclose how I feel?" Many times people find this a hard decision to make because of the risk. We'll have more to say about risk-taking later in this chapter, and also about the positive and negative results of disclosing feelings. Here, we simply want to indicate that people often find it difficult to make direct feeling statements—so we call this a skill.

Finally, you may have difficulty making feeling statements because you are in the habit of substituting opinions, evaluations, or questions for statements of feelings:

> "You have no right to say that!" when you mean "I feel sad when you say that."
>
> "That's a pretty outfit you have on." when you mean "I'm proud to go out with you."
>
> "You shouldn't work late so often! You're married to your job!" when you mean "I feel lonely. I miss you."
>
> "How could you forget my birthday?" when you mean "I felt very disappointed and hurt when you forgot my birthday."
>
> "We have good times together." when you mean "I love you. I enjoy being with you."

How about your own expression of feelings? Can you think of some examples when you have disclosed your feelings indirectly with opinions, evaluations, or questions? How could you have translated them into feeling statements?

We've been talking about the difficulty of making feeling statements to make the point that this involves a skill. But there's another point we want to make about the skill of making feeling statements. As with many other skills in life, we believe this one can be learned and can be developed. It takes practice. We think it's worth the effort. For one thing, trying to state your feelings helps you to keep in touch with your own inner experience, helps you to know yourself. And besides knowing yourself, it helps your partner to know you, too. Feeling statements can bring interest and life to otherwise drab conversations.

Skill #5: Making Intention Statements.

"Sir, what are your intentions toward my daughter?" demands the father as the innocent heroine blushes demurely. The villain, twirling his pointy moustache, says out of the corner of his mouth, "Heh, heh, heh, he'll never know what I'm really after until it's too late!" In drama, an important part of the suspense is for some of the actors, expecially the villain, to keep their intentions a mystery. That keeps the audience involved.

Keeping your intentions a secret in your day-to-day life will probably keep your friends mystified, too. So a very important skill is making intention statements. Intention statements let others know what you want short range or long range.

> "I want to be with you today, but I don't want to spend all our time doing chores."
>
> "I'd like to do my studying in the morning, then catch some sun in the afternoon."
>
> "I'd like to tell you about something interesting that happened to me today."

There's nothing too complicated about making intention statements. You'll know your partner is making intention statements when you hear words like, "I want . . ., I'd like . . ., I intend . . . ." These words let you know where your partner is coming from—what's going on inside of him in terms of his desires.

An intention statement is a way of being *direct* about what you would or would not like for yourself, or about what you would or would not like to do. When we don't state our intentions directly we often go about accomplishing them indirectly. Being direct about our intentions helps in developing plans or understanding actions. Listen to how this sounds:

> "Well, I know you'd like me to play tennis with you this afternoon. I might be able to do it. I suppose I could. If we don't today, maybe we can next week."

Whether this tennis match takes place that day or in the future is really open to question. The key words here are "might," "could," "maybe." These are spongy words that don't state directly what you want. When you hear these words, chances are that the person expressing them is not very likely to act. Note the difference in the following example:

> "Well, I know you'd like me to play tennis with you this afternoon, and I'd like to do that. I think I can, although I've got a lot of work to do. Call me about 3:00. If I can't play, I want to next week."

All of us, from time to time, have hidden intentions. Sometimes these hidden intentions, or hidden agenda, occur because we don't recognize them ourselves. At other times, though, we know our own intentions, but don't want someone else to know them. Often this is because if we say what we want directly we might not get what we want so we go about getting what we want indirectly. If you disclose them, your partner may know more about you than you know about him/her at that point.

For example, in a competitive situation, disclosing intentions may create a disadvantage for the person who clearly puts his intentions on the table. The other person has an advantage—he knows what the first person wants and can work from that in deciding on an action. So, caution and guardedness are often the mode here. But most of your relationships are not competitive ones, and you probably don't want that sort of relationship with your partner. We go even farther. We believe if your intention in relationships is generally to control and direct others, then this book is simply not for you. Our assumption is just the opposite. That is, most people want to participate with others and respond to them. We assume further that most people want intimate relationships in which both partners can be clearly heard and accurately understood. And *that* is the reason we classify intention statements as a very important skill to develop your relationship with your partner.

Just as with feelings, intentions can be in conflict. But these conflicting intentions can be disclosed clearly if you express all the intentions you have:

> "I'd like to be with you, but I want to be with my family tonight, too, because it's my brother's birthday. And I want to spend this afternoon at the library working on my paper."

Again, we'll have more to say about the positive and negative aspects of making intention statements; here we only want to acknowledge that many people do not disclose their intentions.

Skill #6: Making Action Statements.

Making action statements is the sixth skill useful for sharing your awareness with others. An action statement puts words to some of your behavior in a simple, descriptive way. Action statements refer to your own past, current, or future actions, and are often expressed using "being" verbs—was, am, will.

"I tried to call you earlier."

"I will do it."

"I'm listening."

"I was thinking about some stuff at the office. I didn't really hear what you said."

"I believe you."

"I will be there at 5:30."

"I'm thinking about what you just said."

Making action statements simply involves describing your actions, your behavior, to others—what you have done, are doing, or will do. But are they really necessary? Isn't your behavior obvious to everyone? Well, no, as a matter of fact it isn't always. Consider one of the action statements made above, "I'm thinking about what you just said." All that my partner may be able to see is that I am staring off into space and frowning. My partner may or may not be able to guess that I am busily thinking. S/He may think I'm disinterested and avoiding him. Consider the statement, "I tried to call you earlier." This action took place out of sight of my partner. Or "I will call you tomorrow." Now my partner knows what to expect. These statements provide information not otherwise available to him/her.

There's still another reason why action statements have value; they let other people know that you are aware of your behavior. Consider the statement, "I interrupted you." My partner probably noticed the interruption. The information which I provide in my action statement is that I noticed it, too. Disclosing this awareness can be a way of saying that I care about the impact my behavior has on my partner. It's one way of saying, "you're important to me."

A third reason that action statements are important is they let your partner know the meaning you have for your own behavior; what your interpretation is of your own actions.

Meredith and Ted were walking home from the theater. Meredith said, "Ted, I know I was restless tonight and missed most of the play. I want you to know that this wasn't because I was bored with the play. I'm preoccupied with something my sister said to me today, and I had a hard time concentrating on the play."

Meredith has let Ted know she is very much aware that her behavior may have had an impact on him. By describing what she did and interpreting her actions, she showed Ted she wanted him to understand and helped him to clarify what her behavior was all about.

Making action statements is a simple process, and most people make action statements everyday. We call it a skill because it requires (1) awareness of your own behavior, (2) awareness of the possible impact of this behavior on your partner, and (3) remembering to do it, either to provide information to your partner about what you're doing or to let your partner know that you are aware of what you're doing.

Action statements about the future are particularly important because they *involve a commitment* to doing or not doing something. What a difference between saying, "I can . . . ," "I could . . . ," or "I might . . . ," and clearly committing yourself to an action by saying, "I will . . . " Making a future action statement means you let your partner know what s/he can expect from you. And it also provides a check on whether or not you take responsibility for fulfilling your commitments. This can be bothersome, of course, if you're not sure you want to live up to commitments. But if you do, making future action statements can clearly communicate to your partner what you plan to do. Then, by carrying out the action, you can demonstrate that you do live up to your commitments—and this increases trust.

THE RISKS OF SELF DISCLOSURE

Disclosing your self-awareness to others can be risky, particularly disclosing your feelings, your intentions, and your future actions. But when you disclose these things, you are giving your partner important information about yourself.

> Carl and Barbara are sitting on a dock with their feet dangling in the water. Carl says to Barbara, "There is something I've never told you. When I'm with you, I feel excited and happy. I love you. And I feel afraid right now about how you're going to react to all this, but I want you to know how I feel."

You can see in this illustration just how much of himself Carl has disclosed to Barbara. By making several feeling statements and an intention statement, he has disclosed to her important information about his view of their relationship.

Self-disclosing can be experienced as taking a risk, although that's not always the case. A lot depends on the topic, your self-confidence, and the nature of your relationship with the other person. But there are two basic reasons why disclosing can be risky.

First, feeling statements and intention statements can be risky because you don't really know what will happen next; the outcome is uncertain, it's not subject to a pre-planned agenda. And when you make these statements, you put aside attempts to manage and control the situation—or your partner—as you open up and reveal yourself. You may even feel as if you're giving the other an advantage; that disclosing leaves your partner knowing more about you than you know about your partner at that moment. Uncertainty about what will happen next can feel scary. Similarly, future action statements are risky because of the commitment you make. Just as feeling and intentions statements reveal yourself and make you visible, future action statements make you visible. Then, if you don't fulfill your commitment, others can criticize you for your failure, and you'll have a hard time denying you made the commitment.

Secondly, disclosures can be risky because of *what* is being risked, that is, the risk seems to be a risk of injury to your self-esteem or your partner's, or a risk of losing the relationship. If this is what you are risking, then you feel vulnerable. What kinds of questions might Carl have been asking himself as he began disclosing his feelings and intentions to Barbara:

Will she think I'm trying to push her and withdraw?
Will she laugh at me and tell me I sound ridiculous?

One factor determining the degree of risk is the topic. If you disclose your opinions or feelings about a book, that usually does not involve much risk. Opinions or feelings about politics or religion are likely to be somewhat riskier. Your feelings about yourself, about your partner, or about your relationship with your partner are much closer to home—and riskier yet.

As the topic of your disclosures moves closer to yourself, your partner, and your relationship, the degree of risk increases. And, oddly enough, this holds true whether you are disclosing positive or negative feelings. For example, saying "I like you and want to know you better," lays yourself on the line for possible rejection just as much as saying, "I don't like you" does. And both of these statements make you more vulnerable than something like, "I don't like the suit you're wearing."

A second important factor determining the degree of risk of disclosures is your feeling about yourself. If you "just know" that your thoughts and feelings are "stupid" or "silly" or not worth sharing, then you'll expect to be put down and misunderstood if you disclose them. Low self-esteem is not very conducive to risk-taking. But when you have high self-esteem (really value yourself), it's easier to take risks. A person with high self-esteem experiences disclosure as less risky because he anticipates rejection less often than a person with low self-esteem. But that's only part of the picture. The other part is that a person with high self-esteem takes more risks because he depends more on his own self-evaluations. Regardless of others' judgments, acceptances, or rejections, he has the confidence to be himself and to disclose himself without threatening his self acceptance.

A third factor influencing the degree of risk created by disclosures is the nature of the relationship you have with your partner, particularly in terms of trust. How much do you trust his/her commitment to you, his/her caring for you, his/her respect for you, his/her honesty with you? What's the likelihood of your partner taking advantage of you as you make yourself more fully known? If you distrust someone and believe s/he will hurt you, it might be crazy to disclose much about yourself to him/her. That is why it makes sense to be cautious about your disclosures in clearly competitive situations.

At this point you may be telling yourself that disclosures aren't such a great idea. They are risky, especially in close relationships; the ones that matter most to you. But—hold on! Taking risks by disclosing has some enormous advantages, too. The term "risk" not only implies possible loss, it also suggests potential gain.

Most of us are concerned about the possibility of being rejected if we let others know our thoughts, feelings, and intentions. But there's the chance of being *accepted*, too. For example, when you say, "I like you," your partner might say, "I like you, too," or "It sure feels good to hear that." Or when you let your partner know directly what your intentions are, he may decide to cooperate with you. And when he does, you have an ally who is likely to help you a great deal in reaching your goals or satisfying your desires. Few things are more valuable to you in achieving these things than a nurturing and cooperative relationship.

But disclosing has other benefits as well. Even if we try to hide our feelings and intentions, we're usually found out somewhere along the line. Our behaviors and actions often betray us because much of the time they match our feelings and intention. When you disc lose, you don't have to hide who you really are. Moreover, it feels good to take your own feelings and intentions seriously. It's a very strengthening experience. In short, disclosing can help you to value yourself more—help you to build your self-esteem.

And as you begin to disclose with your partner, you are likely to discover another significant benefit: increased trust. Growing, vital relationships don't just happen. These kinds of relationships require large doses of trust. And trust doesn't develop without disclosing personal awareness and letting your partner know you.

Perhaps even more important in developing trust are the commitments you make. That's why future action statements have so much potential for building relationships. When you make a future action statement, you make a commitment to do something or to not do something. Carrying out the action, or refraining from it, gives you the opportunity to show that you do fulfill your commitments; that you are someone to be trusted.

Future action statements contribute to building trust in another way, too. Some people use feeling and intention statements to control and manipulate their partners in a very sophisticated way. But when you make future action statements, you cut through a lot of manipulation by committing yourself to a specific course of action. So this kind of action statement keeps you from abusing the other skills by providing a check. Are you all talk/no action, or do you do what you say you will?

Sometimes partners play a game that could be titled, "If you trust me, I'll trust you." In effect, they're saying, "If you disclose something of yourself or make a commitment, I may be able to take a chance and do the same." But often neither takes the vital first step.

One way of building trust is to start with a tiny bit of disclosure. At first, people usually take small risks. Then as trust grows, it becomes possible to take larger and larger risks. As you disclose more about your feelings and intentions and make bigger commitments, the possibility for trust to develop between you and your partner increases. The more trust, the better the outcome for both of you.

WHY AND WHEN TO SELF-DISCLOSE

The six skills essential to disclosing self-awareness are:

Speaking for self

Making sense statements

Making interpretive statements

Making feeling statements

Making intention statements

Making action statements

Is it really important to be able to verbalize the awareness that you have of yourself? We think so. Consider this. If you fail to disclose who you are in a very direct, verbal way, you are leaving your relationship to chance. Your partner *will* make some guesses about who you are and what you want, based on limited information. He may or may not guess correctly. In lots of ways, what you get out of life depends on others—especially your partner knowing who you are and what you want. Do you want her or him to rely on guesswork?

Disclosure helps you in another way as well. When you begin expressing the awareness you have of yourself directly, you begin to learn more about yourself and more about your relationship.

Tom: "Whenever we come back from Marcia and Al's house I feel irritable and grumpy. They're always very pleasant and lively, and they seem to like us; so I'm not sure what's going on."

Joyce: "I think Marcia wants more attention from you than you want to give. I've noticed she tries to get your attention a lot."

Tom: "Yeah, I think you may have put your finger on it. I feel kind of flattered, and I'd like to just enjoy it, but I'm worrying how it will look to you and how you'll take it. No wonder I feel under a strain when we're at their house!"

When you disclose awareness about yourself to another, you can often clarify some things that have been unclear to you about yourself. That is what happened in that example.

Each of these six skills are useful for sending clear messages, in everyday conversation. But when you use all six at once, stringing them together in complete disclosures, sometimes your conversation is likely to become "heavy." Complete disclosures can make your conversations quite serious. Being "heavy" is okay as long as you want to work on some important issues, and you both agree. But this can be overdone, making every conversation seem as if it were crucial to the development of your relationship.

More specifically, we hope you'll think about using these skills when you have something important to say, or when you think your partner has said something important, *not* as in this example:

"When I see beef steak on the plate I think it must taste good. I start feeling hungrier by the minute and my intention is to eat as much of it as possible."

This is not the best use of these six skills! Compare this with the following examples:

"I really enjoy watching you play with the children. You skip, and run, and laugh right with them. You look like you're enjoying it as much as they are. I like seeing you together and want you to know it."

"When you spend a lot of time with someone else, the way you did at the party last night, I start thinking you're avoiding me and I get furious with you! I find myself wanting to get even with you."

These two examples illustrate appropriate use of these skills in combination. There are times when using one of the skills by itself becomes important. Sometimes one part of your Awareness Wheel becomes especially relevant for the conversation you're engaged in at that time, as in this situation:

"I think we can get this whole situation clarified if I tell you what I want right now, and you tell me what you want."

Finally, a time when all six skills probably will be valuable to you is when you think you misunderstood your partner or are being misunderstood. Often, misunderstandings are corrected by the disclosure of more self-information. For example:

"When I said just now that I didn't like sitting around listening to music with you, I didn't mean I don't want to be with you. I'm sorry you heard it that way. I meant that I want more activity, more exercise, doing something fun outdoors."

Use the skills when something you want to say is important, when you have some particular self-awareness you want to share, or when you think a misunderstanding is taking place.

So far in these first few chapters we have talked about your own awareness and how to express it. In Section II, we'll talk about how to hear and be aware of your partner. But before we do that we have to acknowledge that no one has perfect self-awareness, nor is s/he likely to achieve it. We'd like to spend one more chapter describing what *limited self-awareness* looks and sounds like.

CHAPTER FOUR

COMPLETE AND CONGRUENT SELF-AWARENESS

No one has total awareness. The most that any of us can hope for is to continue the process of becoming more aware throughout our lifetime. As we have said, we believe continuing use of the Awareness Wheel to expand your own self awareness is important because it can enhance your alternatives and help you make more meaningful choices. To better understand the process of becoming aware, it helps to know what limited self-awareness looks, sounds, and feels like.

LIMITED SELF-AWARENESS

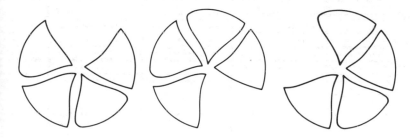

Limited self-awareness exists when one or more dimensions of your Awareness Wheel are not available to you. Remember the five parts of the wheel: your senses, your interpretations, your feelings, your intentions, and your actions. When any one of these is not available to you—has not been brought into your awareness—you are experiencing incomplete self-awareness.

Here, however, we want to make an important distinction. At any point in time, you can really only focus on one thing. For example, when you focus on feelings (emotion), awareness of your thoughts and other inputs diminish. Similarly when you concentrate on looking at something, your hearing slips a bit. When you try mainly to listen to the sounds around you, your visual awareness fades. Try it, where you are right now. Try to look and listen intently at the same time. Do you find yourself shifting slightly from one sense to the other?

The point here is if most of us can really only fully focus on one thing at a time, how can we be "completely aware?" We can't, if we try to be aware of all the dimensions in the Awareness Wheel at the same moment in time. When we speak of "complete" awareness, we are talking about being able to "tune into" all five dimensions (in any order) *within a situation*, but not at the same moment. So, it is possible to have "complete self-awareness" about yourself in a situation, to fill in and use all parts of your Awareness Wheel in a whole and balanced fashion.

When this occurs, you'll find yourself experiencing a sense of completeness, with all the information there and available to you. But when you're lacking some dimension of self-awareness, you'll have a sense of limited or incomplete self-awareness.

As you can imagine, most of us have frequent and extended periods of incomplete awareness. There are some situations where complete self-awareness isn't necessary and limited awareness doesn't create difficulties for you; for example, in a sociable, tension-free situation when you are simply enjoying the interaction. However, even in this kind of situation, increased enjoyment may come from taking in and savoring more of your pleasant awareness.

With incomplete self-awareness, information about yourself is lost or left out. In certain situations, if you leave out one or more dimensions of your Awareness Wheel, the messages you send others will probably be misleading. That's because limited awareness encourages limited disclosure. Here we are talking mainly about interpersonal situations in which misunderstanding is very possible; for example, when you or your partner have strong feelings or intentions.

Look at these situations:

Dad is helping Jimmy with his homework and has just explained how to work a problem in arithmetic. Jimmy indicates he doesn't understand. Dad grits his teeth and brusquely explains again. Jimmy begins to sob. Dad demands to know why Jimmy is crying. "Because you're mad at me," Jimmy sobs. "I am *not* mad at you," Dad exclaims. Jimmy continues to cry and leaves the room. Dad throws down his pencil and paper. "That kid," he groans.

Dad's not in touch with his feelings of frustration and irritation, which he expressed through his behavior. When he denied being mad at Jimmy, this left Jimmy with a perplexing situation: which message should he believe, his Dad's verbal message—"I'm not mad"—or the behavioral message—"I am mad at you"?

Bob and Lynn had just finished supper. Lynn asked Bob if he would mind going shopping with her to look at some new furniture. "Not at all, let's go," Bob replied. But in the course of their shopping trip Bob was irritable, complained of seeing nothing he liked, and made a couple of petty, critical remarks about Lynn. The shopping trip was miserable for both of them.

This episode resulted from Bob's conflicting intentions: (1) he wanted to please Lynn, to do something nice for her by going shopping with her, and (2) he wanted some uninterrupted time for himself that evening to finish a report for the next day. At the time Lynn made her request, Bob was not fully in touch with his second intention and thus failed to take it into account. During the trip he began to feel anxious about the report, and the unacknowledged anxiety surfaced in the form of generalized irritation, spoiling the evening for both of them.

Jill asked Dean if he would mind too much if they skipped the party at their friends' since she had a lot of reading for her classes the next day. Hesitating only a fraction, Dean replied (in a tired, flat tone of voice) that he didn't mind, they could go some other time, or maybe he'd go by himself. Dean stayed at

Jill's apartment, but was quiet and "down" the rest of the evening. When Jill commented on Dean's mood, he replied that nothing was the matter, that he was just tired.

In this case, Dean's feelings of disappointment barely surfaced into awareness before he squashed them. But the feelings didn't just go away. They interfered with his making a choice for himself about the evening. This left him tired and "down" with incomplete awareness.

As you can see in the examples, limited self-awareness can result in unclear and confusing messages. What seems to happen is this. Sometimes you pay too little attention to a particular dimension of awareness. Other times you pay too little attention to another dimension, or leave out a combination of dimensions. Depending on which dimension is neglected, certain behavior patterns tend to occur. And sometimes these behavior patterns create troubles, as in the examples. What we are going to do next is describe several different types of limited awareness that are commonly found and their corresponding behavior patterns.

Leaving Out Sense Data.

People seldom leave out *all* sense data. Rather, what typically happens is that they pay attention to only a small part of the available data. From the limited sense data in their awareness, they jump to a conclusion. Often this results in negative feelings, sometimes pretty strong ones.

One day Larry received a call from a client wanting to know when a contract would be ready. Larry was surprised that the client hadn't received it already because he knew Lou, one of the junior partners, had almost had it done a week before. He told the client he'd look into it. Larry stormed into Lou's office, demanding to know why he hadn't finished the contract—or at least let the client know it would be delayed. Lou explained that he had called the client two days before to tell him about a problem that had arisen. He said he told the client a couple more days would be needed to finish it.

Larry was conclusion-jumping. He paid attention only to what he knew about before, and failed to search for new data to find out whether his conclusion was correct—that Lou hadn't even called the client. Larry's conclusion-jumping led to needless anger which damaged his relationship with Lou. This is a common result from drawing conclusions prematurely.

Leaving Out Feelings.

When we leave our feelings out of our awareness, we still express them, though usually in indirect ways, such as in our tone of voice, body posture, or actions. Frequently the feelings we are not aware of result in our saying or doing something which, in effect, demands that the other person take some action to relieve our feelings, or blames him for them.

> Ray and Jean were reading, watching TV, and waiting up for their teenage daughter to return from a school dance. Ray looked at the clock and exclaimed that it was after midnight and Betty *still* wasn't home! Jean looked surprised. "Maybe I forgot to mention it, but I told Betty she could stay out until one tonight." In a very angry tone, Ray told Jean that she had no business telling Betty she could stay out that late. "What on earth could you be thinking of? She's only fifteen!"

Ray was aware of sensory data (Betty not in; Jean's saying that she gave Betty permission), and his interpretation (Jean is not sufficiently protective of Betty). He was vaguely aware of his intention, that is, to make Jean sorry for what she did and to prevent this happening again. Ray acted on his interpretation and intention. His actions were to criticize; accuse. He left his feelings out of focus. But if he had paid more attention to his feelings (worry, fear, or concern) he would have better understood where he was coming from. If he had directly disclosed these feelings, his communication to Jean might have sounded very different, for example,

> "It really worries me for Betty to be out that late. It really bothers me! I don't like it!"

Jean may still feel criticized, but because he is disclosing his feelings directly she knows his position. So it's easier for Jean to respond constructively to his expressed *worries* than his *condemnation* ("What on earth could you be thinking of?").

Leaving Out Intentions.

Leaving intentions out of your awareness often results in your doing or saying something that you don't really want to.

> John's teenage son, Mike, was telling him about trying out for the basketball team at the high school. As he listened to Mike talk about making the team, John saw how happy Mike was and began to remember with pleasure his own high school days playing on the football team. Pretty soon he interrupted Mike and started telling some stories about games he had played in. After awhile, Mike excused himself and walked out of the room with his shoulders drooping.

John took in sense data (Mike's description of the tryouts), made an interpretation (Mike is really happy), and began to have feelings (pride in Mike and delight in his own memories). But because he wasn't clear about his own intention—to really listen to Mike and enjoy his enthusiasm—he acted largely on the basis of his own feelings, cutting himself off from Mike. Imagine what Mike is thinking: Every time I tell Dad about something good that happens to me, he has to brag about himself.

Not paying attention to your intentions, especially your intentions for your relationship with others, often results in actions which disregard others. Frequently, these actions seem to be based only on your own feelings. It looks to others as if you have no concern for them at all. This can be true when you have positive feelings, as in the illustration above, or when you have negative feelings. With negative feelings and with little awareness of intentions, emotional outbursts often result. This kind of outburst often appears unreasonable and scares others who don't know what to expect next. Impulsive and unpredictable are other words describing behavior when intentions are left out of awareness.

Leaving Out Actions.

Leaving your actions out of your awareness can be just as hard on relationships as any of the others. Although you may be aware of all the other dimensions in your Awareness Wheel, your partner may not be. And, as a result, your actions may be confusing, as in this example.

One of us was talking to a graduate student about a research project we were doing together. The student was telling about problems he was having in data collection. As I listened, I realized that these were major problems, but that I couldn't work on them at that moment because I had to teach a class shortly. I started feeling anxious as the student continued to talk, and became aware that I didn't want to try to solve the problems at that time. Finally, the student began to look uneasy and left. Only later did I realize that I had been fidgeting and speaking abruptly to the student.

In this example, the author was aware of his sensations, interpretations, feelings and intentions, but he wasn't aware of how he translated them into behavior. Had he been aware of it, he could probably have changed the impact it was having on the student; in this instance by an action statement: "I realize I'm fidgeting and cutting you off, but I've got a class that starts shortly. Can we tackle this later?"

Ted was a very sensitive and perceptive guy. He used his Awareness Wheel pretty well. He did a good job of examining sense data, was aware of the conclusions he came to, tuned into his feelings, and knew what his intentions were much of the time. But he had too little awareness of his own actions and the impact of his behavior on others. One evening, he and his buddy, Marshall, were sharing a pitcher of beer. Marshall began talking about some of the difficulties he experienced growing up in a family that moved a lot. He told Ted how hard it had been to make friends and how important it was that Ted was his friend. Taking in the words, and the expression on Marshall's face, Ted concluded accurately that Marshall was reaching out to him, liked him, and wanted some reassurance from him. Ted's immediate intentions were to respond warmly and reassuringly to Marshall. But what Ted actually did was respond with intellectualized comments about the harmful effects of "mass society" and the demands which businesses make on fathers and their families. Marshall assumed he had overstepped the boundaries with Ted. This never got talked about and the two drifted apart over time.

Actions resulting from this type of incomplete self-awareness are frustrating for one's partner. Messages are sent non-verbally which were never intended, such as an "I'm disinterested and don't want to be bothered" message by the author to the student in the first example, and a "Keep your distance" message by Ted to Marshall in the second example. When you are unaware of your own behavior and the impact it has on your partner, the relationship may move in a direction you don't want.

Leaving Out Interpretations.

At this point, you might be asking, "How come you haven't talked about leaving out interpretations?" We haven't because people almost automatically make interpretations. But interpretations do create major problems involving limited awareness, which happen in several ways.

The first way is when you make an interpretation and do not—or cannot—give descriptive sense data (document) to help your partner understand what you mean.

A second common way takes place when you don't pay attention to all the sense data available to you. You jump to a conclusion and simply ignore some of the data. We have discussed this problem so we need not talk about it here except to repeat this point: It's a good idea not to pre-close on your interpretations.

Suppressed interpretations also get involved in limited awareness. For example:

Returning from a visit to her parents' home during spring break, Ann felt restless and annoyed with her parents, but she couldn't tie any specific experiences (sensory data) to what she was feeling. Occasionally she thought she was being put down and treated as though she wasn't capable. But she pushed these thoughts out of her mind and wouldn't permit herself to be aware of her own assessment because it might have led to a question she didn't want to deal with: "What do I want to do about it?" Ann was afraid of altering her relationship with her parents.

It's not uncommon to extend painful feelings by refusing to let your interpretations come fully into awareness. Sometimes we just "refuse to think about it." Recurring headaches, feeling depressed, or frequent irritation at another person suggest some unwanted thoughts may be rattling around somewhere in your head, not being allowed to come into your awareness. Remaining unaware in order to avoid painful feelings associated with an interpretation usually doesn't work very well. Typically, it decreases your chances of doing something effective about the interpretation that's affecting your life, even though you are not fully conscious of it.

   Limited awareness of one's interpretations can stem from other conditions as well:

1. Strong injunctions from childhood against thinking certain thoughts. Here thinking and doing are confused. Rather than owning your awareness (whatever it is) and using all of it to make responsive decisions, your thoughts are censored and unacceptable ones are pushed out of awareness—but not out of your life. The thoughts continue to influence feelings, intentions and actions.

2. Into each situation we carry a host of preconceptions—prior assumptions—developed out of our previous experience with our partners or other people. Over time we develop so many preconceptions and value judgments that it's impossible to be aware of all of them. Still they exert their influence outside our awareness. Some preconceptions are useful, others are not. Sometimes it's important to stop, reflect and get in touch with these assumptions and value judgments.

   George was having difficulty deciding whether he wanted to take an expensive vacation trip or use the money to buy a new car. Kathy interpreted this as "indecisiveness" and felt disappointed in him. Then she recalled reading about "male stereotyping" and the burdensome notion that men must always appear decisive and assertive She could also recall memories of her parents expressing approval of men for being "decisive" go-getters. She was able to relax and join George in discussing the pros and cons.

3. Sometimes we *are* aware of our interpretations but maintain them as "hidden interpretations." In the process we don't let our partner know what we really think about ourself, him/her, or our relationship. When this extends over time, thoughts are withheld out of fear, protection, mistrust, or dishonesty. Hidden interpretations and hidden intentions are "hidden agenda" which spawn conflicting and confusing messages. This form of limited awareness is particularly damaging to your relationship because potentially useful information is being consciously withheld. The growth process is being thwarted by choice.

In short, misinterpretations typically occur with limited awareness—when you ignore information available to you, either information collected by your senses or, perhaps more important, information you have inside yourself (thoughts, feelings, intentions).

THE PROBLEM OF LIMITED AWARENESS

As we have seen, various types of limited awareness affect your relationships with others. It is also true that communication patterns are often linked with different degrees of awareness. All of us operate with limited awareness at various times. Since self-awareness is an ongoing process, you are bound to encounter limited awareness from time to time, even among those of you quite skilled in being self-aware. What we're more concerned about here, however, is a chronic pattern of limited awareness.

Many people typically operate with a specific type of limited awareness. For example, some of us are seldom aware of our feelings. Others pay almost no attention to our intentions. When we get stuck with a chronic pattern of limited awareness, we are likely consistently to act in a way that will cause difficulties in our relationships. As Virginia Satir puts it:[1]

" . . . absolutely clear communication is impossible to achieve because communication is, by its very nature, incomplete. But there are degrees of incompleteness. The dysfunctional communicator leaves the receiver groping and guessing about what he has inside his head or heart."

In talking about limited awareness, we have focused on the dimension or dimensions that are left out. Another way of describing limited awareness is to say it occurs when a person pays *too much* attention to a single dimension of the Awareness Wheel at the expense of other dimensions. This is particularly likely to be the case when s/he becomes stuck in a chronic limited awareness pattern. His/Her awareness is so heavily focused on one dimension that s/he ignores the others. We've had any number of people tell us they get chronically bogged down with their feelings, preoccupied with their thoughts, or locked into their wants to the exclusion of other awareness available to them.

Stop for a moment and think about yourself. Do you have a chronic pattern of limited awareness? With your partner? With other people? What parts do you leave out? What part of your Awareness Wheel do you over-emphasize? Does your pattern become self-defeating?

Shifting to disclosure for a moment, is your pattern less one of limited awareness and more one of failing to disclose your awareness to your partner and others? Which dimension or dimensions do you leave out when you disclose your awareness? In what situations do limited awareness or limited disclosure typically occur for you?

Chronic limited awareness is a serious matter because it creates rigid behavior. It prevents you from being fully aware of all your self-information, information which may be important in your relationship with your partner and with others. Perhaps all of us

[1]Virginia Satir, *Conjoint Family Therapy*, Rev. Edit. (Palo Alto, Calif.: Science and Behavior Books, Inc., 1967), p 73.

have experienced being in a kind of vicious cycle with our partners at some time. We seem to repeat the same pattern time after time without being able to stop it. An important factor in keeping this cycle going may be your own limited awareness. And it can be very hard to break the cycle because, obviously, limited awareness limits your behavior.

Limited awareness has another serious impact. It limits your choices. You can choose to disclose to others only that of which you are aware. If you're only aware of part of your Awareness Wheel, your choices are restricted. For example, if you aren't aware of your feelings, you have no choice about how to disclose them directly. (You probably are expressing them indirectly, however, and this may be confusing your communication.) Self-awareness is necessary before you can make a clear choice about disclosing yourself—how complete and self-revealing you want your communication to be with another person.

There is another important link between self-awareness and disclosures, too. Disclosing to another person helps you become more self-aware and overcome limited awareness. And using the skills for verbally expressing sensations, feelings, etc. helps you to identify and clarify for yourself, as well as your partner, what you are sensing, feeling, etc. In short, self-awareness and disclosing are dynamically related: self-awareness increases your disclosure choices and disclosing can increase your self-awareness. To have "complete" self-awareness in a situation is *to know yourself* in terms of your senses, thoughts, feelings, intentions and actions—all of these.

We've been talking about complete self-awareness as a basis for fostering effective communication. Now let's look at an actual discussion between two people.

The partners in question were engaged to be married. As part of our research, we asked them to discuss the things that each does that irritates the other. The following is a transcription of the audiotape of their discussion. Read the "conversation" part first, and then go back and read the corresponding "process comments."

Conversation	Process Comments	
	Speaking for:	*About:*
Jack: "What's a bad quality of mine?"		
Mary: "I can just think of two things that come to my mind."	Self	My action (thinking)
Jack: "O.K."		
Mary: "Well, you should take a bath more often."	Other	Partner's action
Jack: "Yeah, but, well . . . "		
Mary: "No, I mean you don't smell or anything like that,	Self	My interpretation
but like when we're married I think you should take a bath	Self	Partner's action
every day. Like don't go to bed without washing your face and brushing your teeth."	Other	Partner's action
Jack: "I take a bath every two days."	Self	My action
Mary: "And you watch television so much. Sometimes I	Other	Partner's action
don't think you hear people when they talk when it's on."	Self	My interpretation
Jack: "O.K., mine was . . . "		
Mary: "And I could think of more little things if you want	Self	Partner's action
me to. Like sure I wish you didn't have a little pot belly.	Self	My Interpretation
"And you're a little bit impatient. That should be changed."	Other	Partner's action
Jack: (Jokingly) "Oh, it should, should it?"		

Mary: "Well, you know you're a little bit impatient.	Other	Partner's interpretation
"What irritates you? I covered mine."	Self	My action
Jack: "Well I thought maybe that you get a little upset too easily."	Self	My action (thinks)
Mary: "Yeah. But don't you think I'm improving? A little bit?"	Other	My action
Jack: "Oh, sure, but that doesn't mean you've changed completely yet."	No one	No one's interpretation
Mary: "No, I'm just asking."	Self	My action
Jack: "Yeah, just like the washing bit, don't you think I'm making a better attempt to wash my face and brush my teeth?"	Other	My action
Mary: "Yeah . . . I suppose."		
Jack: "I do it, not every night but I do it when I can remember it."	Self	My action
Mary: "Yeah—What I mean is everyday take a bath.	Self	No one's action
"And you shouldn't wear the same socks two days in a row."	Other	Partner's action
Jack: "Oh, I never do that."	Self	My action
Mary: "Oh, you don't?"		
Jack: "Never—I did last week 'cause I ran out of socks. Never unless I'm out of clean socks.	Self	My action

"What else? Oh, you let emotions enter into your arguments."	Other	Partner's action
Mary: "Yeah, but I don't know if I'll ever change that."	Self	My action

On audiotape the verbal tone quality of this exchange is friendly, suggesting they shared considerable affection for each other. This is probably the first time they had ever directly discussed these things. Now, let's look more closely at the awareness and skill patterns in their discussion. First, most of the time, they are speaking for themselves; however, almost all their irritations are presented by speaking for other—what *you should do,* or think. Second, the entire exchange revolves around interpretation and action statements. We've found this pattern to be quite common. The interpretations are made without sharing their sensory data base (documentation). Action statements about others occur more frequently than action statements about self. Third, no direct feelings are stated. Jack does refer to Mary's emotions, but he does not relate this to his own inner experience. As you probably noticed, intentions are also missing. In short, both Jack's and Mary's awareness appears to be limited.

What difference does all this make? Well, maybe none, unless this is an important discussion from which they would like to learn and grow. Assuming this could be an important discussion for them, what's happening?

Lots of varied and useful information is missing about themselves. As a result, they seem to be in a cyclic pattern, concerned about thinking and doing, while the issues being considered are constantly changing. As a result, there is no new information about any issue, only suggestions about what each should think and do. By not filling out or completing their Awareness Wheels, they provide each other with only limited information from which to make choices and generate resolutions.

INCONGRUENT AWARENESS—AS A GROWING POINT

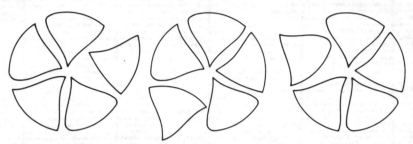

Increasing your awareness is an important step toward becoming more in touch with yourself, toward better understanding where you are and where you're going. But in the process of becoming more aware, you may discover that several of the dimensions of your Awareness Wheel are in conflict. If this happens, we say you are experiencing incongruent awareness. One or two dimensions of your awareness are not congruent with the others. This suggests a growing point—a chance to learn more about yourself, and let your awareness work for you. Look at this example:

> "I thought I would be happy about Jean's promotion (expectation), but I'm sad (feeling). I guess I hadn't been fully aware of it till now, but I think her promotion will mean we'll have less time to be together."

In this example, the partner becomes aware of conflict between how he thought he would react to Jean's promotion—a happy event—and his actual feeling response—sadness. This sent him searching for *what else* the promotion meant to him; that is, to searching for another interpretation he was making, but something of which he had not been completely aware. He was able to identify it: What Jean's promotion *also* meant to him was that they would have less time together. This is an example of incongruence between *feelings* and *interpretations* (expectations).

Incongruency between feelings and expectations is quite common. We expect to feel one way but discover that we feel another way. Having expectations about how we *should* feel often results in incongruence, because feelings are spontaneous and can't be programmed.

Let's turn now to another type of incongruent awareness, involving incongruency between *intention* and *action.*

At the noon hour, Jim unexpectedly meets his wife near his office. He wants to give her a hug and kiss, but he doesn't. He becomes aware that he is not doing something he wanted to do. What was going on? Silently Jim started to sort things out for himself. "I guess I think people will stare, and I don't want that. I'd feel embarrassed if people stared. I never thought I was so sensitive to 'what people think'!" Jim knows more about himself now than he knew before.

Incongruence between intention and action also is rather common. Usually it is the result of conflict between two intentions: (1) the intention you're aware of but fail to carry out, and (2) the intention you *do* carry out but of which you are not aware. It is the lack of awareness of the more powerful intention which produces the experience of incongruence. In the example, Jim didn't realize how much he wanted to avoid being stared at until he began sorting out the incongruence between wanting to do something and not doing it. When your intentions are not in conflict, you can put your actions in line with your intention. If you have difficulty doing so, look carefully at *other* intentions that might be operating. Your actions are an important clue to these other intentions. What are the other intentions which might be operating in the following examples?:

You want to get up early on Saturday, but you turn the alarm off and go back to sleep.

You want to study for an exam, but you read a book or watch TV.

You want to let your partner know how much s/he means to you, but you say nothing.

A third common type of incongruent awareness involves discrepancy between *sensations* and *interpretations.* When something you see or hear surprises you, you can be sure that you had expected something different. Sometimes the experiencing of surprise provides the first inkling that you had *expected* anything at all. For example:

> Jack was surprised one day when he overheard his partner make a critical remark about him to a friend. It wasn't the content of the criticism that surprised him—she had made the same criticism to his face several times. What surprised him was the fact that she would say this to a friend. When he reflected upon it, Jack realized that he did not *expect* Diana ever to say anything critical about him to a mutual friend, and furthermore that he expected the same of himself in talking about Diana. Sorting it out, Jack became aware of a "rule" about their relationship which was operating for him: neither partner should criticize the other to "outsiders."

Frequently you may experience a discrepancy between a *feeling* and *intention;* this is another type of incongruent awareness. The feeling and the intention just don't seem to go together: you know what you want but your feelings keep you from acting on your intentions. For example, what you want may change some aspect of your relationship and this scares you. Your actions are blocked by your feelings. Achieving congruence here might involve increasing your awareness of other parts of your wheel, or perhaps changing your interpretation of the situation. It might involve changing your intentions, or possibly facing your fear head on with action. However you choose to move toward congruence, a precondition for making a choice is an awareness of incongruency between your feelings and intentions.

COMPLETE AND CONGRUENT AWARENESS

Limited self-awareness means you have incomplete access to the richness of your own inner experience. Since you can only *choose* to act upon those things you are aware of, limited self-awareness means limited choices about what to do and about what you can choose to communicate to your partner. Many people typically operate with a specific type of limited awareness, that is, some pay little attention to their feelings and intentions, others don't realize how they put them into action. A chronic pattern of limited awareness often leads to a behavior pattern which causes difficulty in relationships.

Self-awareness *can* be increased and heightened—by getting in contact with your Awareness Wheel, *beginning with any dimension.* Fill it out completely and disclose yourself to your partner. Self-awareness and self-disclosure are dynamically interrelated— self-awareness increases your disclosure choices and disclosing can increase your self-awareness.

The process of expanding your awareness may involve risk and sometimes pain because you may discover an incongruence which requires you to do something. It may mean changing some action or value, or aligning your expectations for yourself and your partner in a different way. It may involve changing your intentions. And feelings will change in ways that cannot be predicted beforehand.

So there are risks. But we believe there are great risks in limited awareness, too. If you could look inside the body of someone suffering with incomplete or incongruent awareness, you'd find muscular tensions, headaches, chest pain, elevated blood pressure, upset stomach, disturbed sleep patterns, and very often an extra amount of fatigue. That is the price you pay. It takes energy to limit your awareness and maintain incongruities, and a fight within yourself. And that struggle, that stress, reaches out to your relationships, too.

We don't think you have to pay this price. Rather, we think you can use your expanded awareness, even when it includes incongruence, as a growth opportunity. You can use it to make modifications in yourself or your relationship to bring the dissonant dimensions back into alignment. We think you'll find that working toward complete and congruent awareness will enrich your life. Besides the obvious benefit of increasing your knowledge of yourself and keeping you more in contact with who you are, we believe you'll find other substantial benefits: greater spontaneity in your actions, feelings of self-acceptance and calm, and a greater sense of purpose and direction in your life.

KEY IDEAS FROM SECTION ONE

1. Self awareness is the process of tuning into self-information.

2. Your Awareness Wheel has five different kinds of self-information:

   Sensations

   Interpretations

   Feelings

   Intentions

   Actions

3. Disclosing your self-awareness involves skills:

   Speaking for self

   Making sense statements

   Making interpretations

   Making feeling statements

   Making intention statements

   Making action statements

4. Communication problems develop when your disclosure of self-awareness is incomplete or incongruent.

AWARENESS OF OTHER

To this point we've talked about, your own self-awareness and expressions of it. We've emphasized this part of communication because what you want to communicate to others often involves information about yourself, the information in your Awareness Wheel. Consequently, it's important to know what the information is before you begin to communicate with another person.

But communication involves more than you. It involves you and your partner. If you simply gave information to another person while he sat and listened, communication would be limited at best. In fact, it would really just be a monologue. More often you share information with your partner and s/he shares information with you. In short, the two of you participate together in a dialogue.

Flexible, effective communication in a dialogue involves more than skills in expressing self-awareness. Two other things are needed support in helping your partner identify and express his own self-awareness, and the ability to accurately hear your partner talk about his awareness.

The chapters in this section are about dialogue—the exchange of information between people. These chapters will discuss skills useful in helping others exchange information with you, and some of the factors influencing people's willingness to receive information from others.

CHAPTER FIVE

TO SHARE A MEANING

Self awareness is one thing. Awareness of others is another. When you're self-aware, you know what's going on in your own Awareness Wheel—your senses, thoughts, feelings, intentions, and actions. As we have seen, using the Awareness Wheel and expressing self-awareness can put you more in tune with yourself.

Awareness of others means tuning into their immediate experience—their Awareness Wheel. When you are intimately and accurately aware of someone else's sensations, thoughts, feelings, intentions, and the meaning of their actions, you are truly aware of him/her. But just as it's not easy to become completely aware of yourself in a situation, it's tough to be completely aware of another person as well. In fact, it may be impossible. But you can become more aware of others.

INCREASING AWARENESS OF OTHERS

Increased awareness of others is possible in several different ways. One way is to pay close attention to the sense data you are receiving from the other person and to the interpretations you are making from these data. To do this, it's often helpful to use the Awareness Wheel as a guide. You can almost pose a series of questions for yourself:

"What do I think the other person is sensing (seeing, hearing, etc.)?"

"What do I think he's thinking—what interpretations is he drawing from his sensations?"

"What do I think he's feeling?"

"What do I think his intentions are—what does he want to have happen?"

"What do I think his actions mean—what is he doing?"

Stop for a minute and try it yourself. Think back to a recent encounter you had with a person important to you, and answer those five questions. Next, think about how you processed the situation. What did the person do that led you to conclude he was sensing something? Was it his eye movements, body posture or what? What did s/he do or say that suggested to you s/he was thinking something? How about his/her feelings? Did you focus on his/her tone of voice, his/her words, breathing rate or something else in making your interpretation about what he was feeling? What data did you use in drawing conclusions about his intentions and the meaning of his/her actions?

How did you do? Were you able to clearly identify the sense data *you used* in inferring what he sensed, thought, and so forth? Even though we may not be clear about the data, we all constantly draw conclusions about other people's behavior. Of course, we have no other choice—living with others demands that we do this. The skill is in knowing how we arrived at our conclusions.

Luckily, most of us are pretty accurate in the assumptions we make about others much of the time. But sometimes we aren't. How many times can you remember something like this happening to you?

Other person: "How could you do this to me? Didn't you know I would feel . . . (or, I wanted to . . .)?"

You: "Well, I thought you . . . "

It's the rare person who hasn't had this experience many times.

When we draw conclusions about what others are thinking or feeling, we make guesses. As noted above, much of the time our guesses are pretty good, but sometimes they're way off base. How accurate they are is likely to depend on how much information is available to us, including both information in the present situation and information from our past experiences. Using the Awareness Wheel to observe the other person can be helpful in increasing your awareness of him, but the information you then have will probably still be pretty limited. To increase your information, you need to become more active. And that's where some other skills come in.

Skill #7. Checking Out.

Checking out helps you *discover* or *clarify* your partner's awareness. This is the skill of asking the other person what's going on in his Awareness Wheel.

> "Half the time tonight you've been laughing and telling stories, and the other half of the time, you've been staring into space. I don't know what to make of your actions. What's going on?"

Here the speaker is sharing his awareness and asking about his partner's awareness. In this particular message, the speaker is doing three things: (1) documenting what he is seeing and hearing by making a sense statement, (2) stating that he doesn't have an interpretation, and (3) asking for information. So his partner has a better idea of where he is coming from and what he is asking for.

This is quite different from demanding or challenging when you might say, for example, "What's going on with you tonight anyway!"

The simplest way to "check out" something is to add a who, what, where, when, or how type question to any dimension of your partner's Awareness Wheel. This then becomes a *process* question—asking about "what's happening?"

1. Who do you *want* to include?

2. What do you *think*?

3. What are you *doing*?

4. Where did you *hear* that?

5. How do you *feel*?

These questions can be very useful in helping your partner describe what he is experiencing. They are open questions that allow your partner to disclose his awareness, as he's experiencing it. How you ask any question, even which question you ask, springs from your own intentions. If you sincerely want to expand your awareness of your partner's experience, you can ask him directly.

The action of checking out by asking questions is abused when it keeps attention off yourself—when it serves to hide your awareness by raising questions about your partner's awareness. Questions also can be used to disguise statements about yourself. Example:

"Don't you think it would be better if we both went?" (Rather than, "I want to go with you.")

"How come you don't do it my way?" (Rather than, "I'm angry because you won't do it my way.")

"Aren't you interested?" (Rather than, "I don't think you're interested.")

These kinds of questions are frequently called *closed* or leading questions. They don't allow your partner much choice.

"Why" questions, usually have the same effect. They ask questions that are frequently impossible to answer, searching for cause, usually in order to assign blame. These questions hold somebody else responsible for what happened.

"Why did you do that?"

"Why did that happen?"

"Why do you feel that way?"

In short, "why" questions are better avoided because they seldom lead to clear understanding of a situation. On the other hand, checking out with who, what, when, where, and how questions can be very helpful in clarifying understanding. These questions can be answered. (But watch your intentions for using them.)

Another effective use of checking out involves letting your partner know what conclusion you have drawn, then asking him whether it is accurate.

"Half of the time tonight you've been laughing and telling jokes, and the other half you've been staring into space. It makes me think that you're laughing to avoid some sadness or something. Is that true?"

"When you don't respond to my suggestion about the weekend, I think you really don't want to go along with it. Is that right?"

"I see you nodding as if you agree with what I am saying. Do you?"

In each example, the speaker has drawn a conclusion about his partner's thoughts, feelings, or intentions *and* documented how he arrived at the conclusion. Then he asks whether his conclusion fits with his partner's experience. In a sense, this kind of check-out lets your partner know you have drawn a conclusion, that it's only a tentative one, and that he has the final say on what he's experiencing.

A closely related kind of checking out shows your partner that you are paying attention and have received a message—but your interpretation is open and subject to change because you put your interpretation in the form of a question, waiting for your partner's confirmation.

> "You're excited about something, but are having a hard time putting it into words?"

> "You'd like to be with me tonight, but don't particularly care what we do?"

> "You want to ask me about something, but don't know how to start?"

The important message to communicate in using a reflective check-out is that your interpretation (about your partner's thoughts, feelings, intentions and actions) is indeed a tentative one. What's missing is documentation of your interpretation, and, as a consequence, your partner may not know where you are coming from. Because of this, it is important to keep your interpretation tentative, letting him say if it fits or not.

Besides not allowing your partner final authority over your interpretation of his actions, there is another possible danger in using reflective check-outs, and that is, mind-reading, wild guessing, or "psyching the other out." For example:

> *Mary:* "I really get tense when I'm with my parents too long."

> *Bert:* "You're angry and tense because you want their approval and you're afraid they don't approve of the way you're living?" (Speaking for other covered with a question.)

> OR,

> *John:* "When I'm with you, most of the time I feel happy and satisfied. But I feel uncomfortable sometimes because I don't know how you're feeling about me."

> *Carol:* "It sounds as though you really like me, but you'd like me to say it first?"

Mind reading, wild guessing, and "psyching the other out" usually stem from a couple of sources. First, you might have hidden intentions, and you are trying to get your partner to see things your way. Secondly, you might be adding meanings instead of listening carefully and staying close to the data (what you see and hear). The misuse of reflective checking out usually is resented by your partner because it's a way of speaking for him, confusing rather than clarifying messages. This can be avoided by paying close attention to your intentions and keeping track of the data you are receiving. You may find, as you document your interpretations, that you begin to include sense statements in your messages, thereby helping your partner to better understand the basis for your interpretations. Most important, when using reflective check-outs, however, is to keep your interpretation tentative, and let your partner know it's tentative.

To summarize, there are a number of ways to "check out" your partner's awareness. The skill mainly involves asking a question about a specific dimension of his awareness. This helps you increase your information about where your partner is coming from, and thereby can increase your understanding of him. Checking out isn't useful only because it helps you, however. Sincere checking out demonstrates your commitment to your partner's well-being—you are letting him know that you're interested in him and care about what he thinks or feels or wants. So check-outs can contribute a great deal to good feelings in your relationship.

Check-outs and questions in general share one major danger, though: the focus can be shifted entirely away from you. Check-outs can be used to hide your self from your partner. At the extreme, a series of check-outs can change a dialogue into an interview, with you asking the questions and your partner answering. When this happens, things get one-sided. Your partner's taking all the risks. You can avoid interviews quite readily, however, by responding to your partner with process statements from your own awareness—about "what's happening" with you.

THE SHARED MEANING PROCESS

Paying close attention to your partner and checking out are two ways to make your hunches about what's going on in your partner's Awareness Wheel more accurate. However, there is a third way to achieve a high degree of accuracy. This involves general skills, and is so important that we present the shared meaning process here in a section all its own.

Perhaps the most typical way in which a shared meaning begins is when a receiver is not sure he is "receiving" his partner's message accurately:

Sender	Receiver
	"I'm not sure I'm understanding what you're saying. Can I run back what I'm hearing?"
"Okay."	
	"I'm hearing that you want me to let you know what I think about things more often. Is that right?"
"That's it. I'd like you to share what's on your mind."	

Note that what the receiver is doing here is very similar to a check-out. However, he is doing a couple things in a slightly different way. First, by his initial intention statement (I want to make sure I'm hearing you right), he lets his partner know he wants to achieve accuracy. Second, he reports back in his own words the message he heard from his partner, and asks for confirmation or clarification.

A second common way in which the shared meaning process is begun is when a sender wants to be certain he is being, or will be, understood. So he simply states his *intention* to share a meaning, sends the *message* he wants to share and *asks* his partner to acknowledge his message by reporting back (in his own words) what he has just heard.

Figure 5-1

REGULAR CONVERSATION

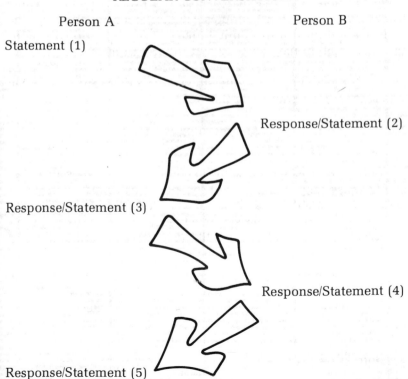

Person A   Person B

Statement (1)

Response/Statement (2)

Response/Statement (3)

Response/Statement (4)

Response/Statement (5)

In either receiver-initiated or sender-initiated situations, the goal is essentially the same: to insure that message sent equals message received. The shared meaning process is begun when either the receiver wants to be certain he is understanding the other, or the sender wants to be certain he is being understood. The process involves listening attentively and tuning in to each other, trying to insure understanding about what you sense, think, feel, want, are doing, or will do. Both partners become actively involved in making the process work.

Let's look at the shared meaning process in a little more detail. We'll begin by contrasting it with a regular conversation. As we see in Figure 5-1, a regular conversation seems to flow forward.

The conversation typically involves statements and responses which build upon the same topic, with a shift in topic occurring periodically.

On the other hand, a shared meaning process involves *going backwards* for a few minutes. Rather than continuing the conversation in forward motion, one partner intentionally stops the conversation momentarily and involves the other person in reporting back the messages he has just received. In the end, each person knows he has understood the other and has been understood. Here's an example:

Bob: "I'd like to share a meaning with you."

Judy: "Okay."

Bob: "I've been getting some uncomfortable feelings about the Thanksgiving thing we've been planning and I really don't want to go. To me the trip is not worth two days of driving with the kids, and all the hassles involved, and yet I think you want to go to see your folks. So I'd like to explore some alternatives a bit. What do you hear me saying?"

Judy: "I hear you saying that you've been feeling some discomfort thinking about the trip to my parents at Thanksgiving, even though you think I want to go. Because of the difficulty driving with the kids, etc., you don't want to go and you'd like to look at some other possibilities."

Bob: "Right. That's it."

As you can see, the shared meaning process focuses only on a portion of an on-going dialogue. It involves three steps:

Step 1. The sender expresses his *intention* to share a meaning, *sends* his message and *asks* the receiver to report back what he has just heard.

Step 2. The receiver *acknowledges* the sender's original message by reporting back in his own words what he has just heard. Here the receiver is careful not to add any of his own meanings (e.g., what he *thinks* the sender is saying).

Step 3. The sender then either *confirms* the accuracy of the receiver's acknowledgement, or, if necessary, *clarifies* it to help the receiver understand it accurately. Note that clarifying does not mean changing the original message.

The sender-initiated shared meaning process involves a minimum of three steps. Sometimes, however, it takes five, seven, or more loops backwards to insure that message sent equals message received. As we noted before, the process may begin either at Step 1, with the sender initiating the process, or at Step 2, with a receiver taking the initiative. (If the receiver initiates, it involves a minimum of two steps.) Figure 5-2 shows what the shared meaning process looks like. The conversation actually moves backwards. The conversation does not move forward again on the topic until the sender has confirmed the accuracy of the receiver's acknowledgement.

Let's look at some more shared meanings. These are from tape recorded discussions of partners we have known over the past few years.

Phil: "I don't think it's heavy, but I just wanted to tell you that I'm sort of aware of having passed by you a couple of times in the past year and wanted to kind of get back again, some way."

Julie: "Hang on a minute and just let me see if I understood what you're saying. We've bumped into each other a couple of times this year and you're wanting to see more of each other again?"

Figure 5-2

SHARED MEANING PROCESS

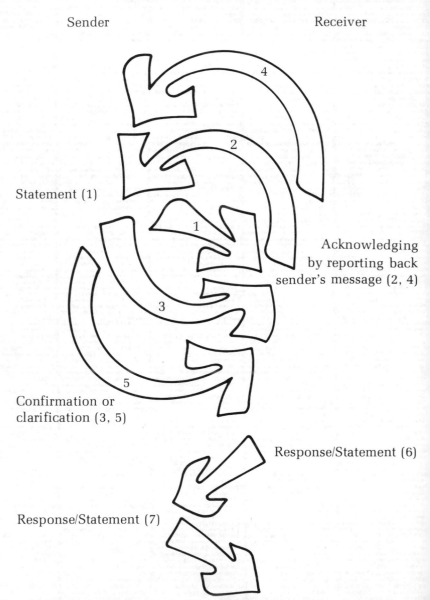

Phil: "Yeah, that's what I was saying, but there's a little more, too. It's exciting to see you tonight, but I'm not sure that it will work out any more off into the future, you know? I'd like it to, I think, but I'm not sure that it will."

Julie: "Let me try that. I'm hearing that you're feeling very good about our being together tonight, but you have some doubts about whether we could build upon this. And the way you're hesitating, I hear you saying you're not certain you want to try, although you would sort of like to. Is that it?"

Phil: "That's right."

Julie: (Continuing dialogue with own response) "I have the same response and also the same doubts, Phil. Some really exciting things have happened for me in the last year, and being with you brings back some really strong memories."

In this example, Julie (the receiver) began the process at Step 2 by indicating she thinks Phil has said something significant and by telling him she wants to understand what he is saying. Julie acknowledges his message by reporting in her own words the message she heard in Step 2. At Step 3, Phil confirms that Julie has accurately understood his message, and sends a second message which builds on the first message. Julie acknowledges this message, too, by describing what she is hearing. Lastly, note that Julie does not go beyond Phil's message to report her own feelings and thoughts until she accurately understands the message.

Let's take another example:

Joan: "Right now we are both really into a busy life style doing our own things, and I've found out that the thing that has been sustaining me is our basic commitment to each other and our relationship. So the other night when you told me you were having troubles with our lack of intimacy, and you said you didn't know if you could continue in the marriage, my trust level dropped drastically, and it was really a frightening experience. Uh, because the other thing is last summer we made sort of a recommitment to our relationship and at that point you said you would never use that threatening to leave in anger. And so I'm really lost; my trust level has dropped. That's the way I can describe it. What do you hear me saying?"

Bill: "I hear you saying that you were frightened by my saying, in our argument the other night, that I wasn't sure about our relationship. Also, that you were helped by the trust you had for our commitments to each other, but my threat the other night really hurt that. Is that right?"

Joan: "Uh-huh, but a really important part of it is that you said you wouldn't threaten me just out of anger."

Bill: "Okay. So the damage to your trust came because you thought I was very serious about leaving because I had agreed not to threaten you simply because I was angry. Is that it?"

Joan: "Yeah, you're reading me right."

Here, Joan (the sender) has initiated the shared meaning process at Step 1 by asking Bill to acknowledge her message. (Her message was very long and consequently hard to feed back accurately.) The process continues by Bill taking responsibility for clearly understanding Joan's initial message and not adding to it. He reports back only what he's heard. At Step 3, Joan confirms the accuracy of part of his message, but also restates an important part (to her) which he missed. In Step 4, Bill paraphrases the missing part, which Joan confirms (Step 5). After the shared meaning is achieved, the conversation continues:

Bill: "Well, I've got really mixed feelings about that. On the one hand, I feel bad that you're not trusting me and our relationship because I want you to. But on the other hand, I'm surprised that I shocked you because I thought that there was enough conflict going on between the two of us that you must recognize all that struggle and tension in our relationship. So part of me is glad that I finally got a message of frustration through to you, but I feel bad that it had to be a message that really set you back in terms of trusting our relationship. How are you reading me?"

Joan: "I'm hearing that when you came out with that Sunday night, that was coming out of your frustration. And that you're glad the message finally got through to me, but you're also sorry that it shocked me and hurt my trust in your commitment to us."

Bill: "Yes. (and moving beyond the shared meaning) But I'd like to add something, too. I'm very aware that I don't think like that except in extreme frustration when we're in an argument. And I think it's when I don't think I'm getting through to you, and then I really do think it and feel it and I'm not making it up. But I don't think my intention is to hurt you or shock you, but at the moment it seems very real. But I'm also very glad that I'm not at that spot very often."

Joan: "Oh, that feels better to me. And I guess I knew in my head that that was most likely true because that's been a pattern in the past. But emotionally it devastated me because of what I thought we had agreed not to use that anymore, both of us."

Bill: "Well, that agreement is foggy to me."

Joan: "Okay, let's talk about that again. But the other thing is when you say that, it hits the mark, you know. I really hear you loud and clear, but it's really a high price to pay."

This time, after achieving a shared meaning, Bill (the sender) begins a second shared meaning process, trying to help Joan understand his feelings and point of view. And Joan (as receiver) acknowledges his message, retaining a focus only on his message. In turn, Bill confirms her accuracy, then immediately moves beyond the shared meaning by adding to his message and the conversation continues.

This continuing example illustrates the dynamic and transitory nature of the shared meaning process. It shows clearly that achieving a shared meaning is not necessarily a goal in and of itself. Rather, it is simply a means toward increasing both partners' understanding of each other's point of view at important points in a conversation. When a shared meaning is achieved it gives both partners the confidence that understanding has occurred, and that the conversation can move forward from a point of understanding rather than from a point of misunderstanding. The example also illustrates one other important point: understanding does not necessarily lead to agreement. In the example, Joan and Bill did not, at the end, agree not to threaten each other with leaving the relationship any more. Whether they do reach an agreement on this will depend on what happens when they talk more about it. But even without agreement, they moved a long way toward clearing up some significant tension in their relationship simply by showing a willingness to and the ability to achieve several important understandings. By understanding each other they demonstrate acceptance of, but not necessarily agreement with, each other.

After seeing several examples of the shared meaning process, how can you know a shared meaning has been achieved? First, if you were a third person watching the process, you would usually see both partners nod their heads, give some kind of facial recognition (often a smile) and move their bodies spontaneously, without hesitation. In short, they are naturally signalling to each other that the shared meaning process is complete. That is, *both the sender and the receiver are satisfied that the message the sender sent has been accurately received and understood.* If there is any hesitation (in facial expression or body movement) the meaning is probably only partially shared. When two people achieve a shared meaning, both feel good about it, even though they may have different points of view about the message.

SKILLS INVOLVED IN THE SHARED MEANING PROCESS

All of the basic communication skills discussed in the first section support the shared meaning process because this process can be used to share any of the dimensions of the Awareness Wheel. We've noticed that it's easier for meanings to be shared if the messages sent contain more than two dimensions of the sender's Awareness Wheel, briefly stated. When several dimensions are included more complete information is made available and the receiver doesn't so easily fall into guessing about what's being said.

Compare sharing this meaning,
"I'm confused right now."

with

"I'm confused (feeling) right now, about what I just said (action) and I'd like you to help me (intention) clear things up (action)."

Besides briefly including more than one dimension of the Awareness Wheel in a message, perhaps the two most important skills to use are speaking for self and documenting. Speaking for self is crucial because both persons are reporting their own messages—that is, the sender is stating his message and the receiver is reporting the message that he has received. If either the sender or receiver tries to speak for the other, the goals of helping each other achieve understanding are likely to be undermined. Documenting (describing) by making sense statements is important for the receiver in particular, as it is a way of making clear to the sender what messages the receiver has been hearing and seeing.

Three new skills are also used in the shared meaning process: stating intention and asking for acknowledgement; acknowledging; and confirming/clarifying.

Skill #8. Stating Intention and Asking for Acknowledgement.

The sender uses this skill when he wants to share a meaning. When a sender wants to initiate a shared meaning he signals this in two ways. First, by stating his intentions ("I want to share a meaning"), and secondly, by asking his partner to acknowledge what he's heard ("What do you hear me saying?"). For example:

"I want to tell you something that's important to me and then have you tell me what you heard me say."

"I'd like to know what you are hearing me say because this is important to me."

"I'm not sure how I'm coming across. What do you hear me saying?"

This last example illustrates how a sender might initiate a shared meaning when he thinks some previous statements are being misunderstood.

Asking for acknowledgement serves as a kind of signal to your partner to let him know that you want to share a meaning. But it does more than this. Your signal tells him that you want information from him, either general information concerning the whole message or more specific information. The sender can ask for more specific acknowledgement by making his request more specific, for example, by focusing on one dimension of the Awareness Wheel.

> "I have some pretty strong feelings about this. I'd like to know what feelings you hear me expressing."

> "I'm trying to say what my intentions are. What do you hear me saying they are?"

Other kinds of statements can serve as cues for the receiver, but they may not help the receiver feed back information very effectively. For example, take the statement, "Do you understand me?" Here the sender is asking the receiver to make a judgment that *only the sender* himself can really make, rather than asking the receiver to *demonstrate* his understanding by reporting back what he has heard. When the receiver reports back the message he's receiving in his own words, he shows the sender what he is understanding. Tape recorders can play back messages accurately, but they don't "understand." This is the reason that we insist that the receiver repeat the message in his own words. This helps the sender judge whether his message has been understood as intended or not, and whether or not he needs to clarify.

When the sender finishes a statement by saying something like, "do you agree?", or "what are your feelings about that?", he will probably not get a shared meaning started. These kinds of questions do not ask for understanding. Rather, they encourage a response, like "yes," "no," or "sort of." The receiver is asked to respond rather than to demonstrate understanding.

Skill #9. Acknowledging the Sender's Message.

Acknowledging the sender's message is done by the receiver, reporting back to the sender what he saw and heard in his own words. In a sense, it simply involves the receiver giving back (paraphrasing) the sender's original message. The language used is:

"I hear you saying . . ."

"I'm hearing . . . "

This kind of language indicates you will be reporting back the sender's message. Other language, which is often used, moves the conversation away from a shared meaning:

"Are you saying . . . (This is checking out, not stating what you're hearing.)"

"You are saying . . . (This is speaking for other.)"

"I think you're saying . . . (This is interpreting, guessing, imagining.)"

The emphasis in acknowledging is upon completeness, but the receiver reports back only parts of the message actually stated (the intention, feelings, etc.). As part of being complete, the receiver often makes sense statements to clarify what he's seeing as well as hearing, especially when he is relying on visual data or vocal qualities (e.g., pitch, rate of speech, hesitations) in feeding back messages. For example, in acknowledging Phil's message Julie documented in the following way:

> "And the way you're hesitating, I hear you saying you're not certain you want to try, although you would sort of like to."

There is a danger in attempting to be complete, however. The danger is that the receiver will try to read additional meanings into the message or add things that weren't said. When you're doing this you're inferring meaning, adding messages to the sender's original statement. To avoid guessing, stick close to the data; to exactly what you're seeing and hearing.

In a receiver-initiated shared meaning, acknowledging gets a bit more complicated. Not only does the receiver try to report back the sender's message, but he also gives a signal to the sender that he wants to use the shared meaning process. Julie also provides an example of this when she said to Phil:

> "Hang on a minute and just let me see if I understand what you're saying."

Sometimes it's useful to begin a receiver-initiated shared meaning by a disclosure of the receiver's feelings. For example:

> "I'm getting sore. But maybe I'm not hearing you right. What I understood you to say was . . . Is that what you meant?"

It often seems necessary to self-disclose some strong feelings—if you have some—before the two of you can move into the shared meaning process. If you attempt to move into the process without disclosing strong feelings when they're present, it may cause your acknowledgement to sound blaming or accusing.

Making the assumption that you know what the sender meant, and then acting on this assumption often leads to arguments, misunderstanding, and anger. Disclosure of feelings, combined with acknowledging, can often cut off this kind of angry exchange and facilitate moving into a shared meaning.

Skill #10. Confirming/Clarifying.

This skill can be very easy to use if the receiver is accurate in his acknowledgement. All the sender has to do is say something like, "that's it," "you got my meaning," "you're with me," etc. But *failure to confirm or clarify* leaves the receiver dangling—feeling uncertain and frustrated. He gets no cue from the sender whether or not he's accurate. Lederer and Jackson suggest that you can drive your partner "nuts" by failing to confirm or clarify the accuracy of his feedback.[1]

When the receiver's acknowledgement is not entirely accurate, it gets more complicated. What the sender needs to do when this happens is indicate what part of the acknowledgement is accurate and what part is not. For example:

"You're reading my feelings right, but I don't think you caught the part I was saying about my intentions." (Then repeat the missing part.)

Or if the acknowledgement is completely accurate, but incomplete, the sender can clarify as Joan did with Bill:

"Uh-huh, but a really important part of it is that you had said you wouldn't threaten me just out of anger."

Finally, if the receiver is 'way off base, or the sender can't remember his original message, the sender may have to restart the whole process.

"No, I don't think you've got my message. Let me start again." (Then rephrase the original message.)

[1] W. J. Lederer and D. D. Jackson, *The Mirages of Marriage* (New York: Norton, 1968).

Remember, sometimes it is necessary to recycle the shared meaning process several times until the sender knows the receiver understands what he said (by acknowledgement) and the receiver is assured (by confirmation) that the sender has accurately heard and understood.

We would caution you here. When the sender attempts to repeat or clarify his original message, there is a temptation for the sender to add to or change his original message. This can create enormous difficulties because the receiver gets more confused. It's important that the sender remember his original message and restate it accurately. If the sender, for some reason, is changing his original message, it's essential that he clearly indicate he is changing the meaning, as in this example:

> "I didn't say exactly what I meant before so I want to start this over. What I mean is . . . "

USES OF THE SHARED MEANING PROCESS

Shared meanings are for important issues between partners. They can be very helpful in building your relationship. *Use the shared meaning process when you have an important message you want to share with your partner;* when you want to be sure your partner understands the message. And use it *when you think you or your partner may be misunderstanding each other.* Other times when the shared meaning process seems particularly useful are:

1. As a way of helping the sender better understand his own message. Many people report that hearing their message reflected back makes it clear to them the other person accurately heard their message, yet they discover they have left an important part of their message out. They *thought* it but failed to *state* it.

2. As a way of letting the other know that you're listening.

3. As an aid to myself is listening attentively, to help me pay attention. Both #2 and #3 require judgment because overuse of the shared meaning process can nullify its effectiveness.

4. When my partner has a personal concern (not involving me) that he wants to think through with my help as a "sounding board." I'm acting as a resource person, helping him sort out or get in touch with his own ideas, feelings, intentions. Reporting back messages received can be very helpful to him/her.

5. When you want to send a positive intimate message about "something I like about you, and the impact it has on me." For example:

   "I like your tenderness, especially when a tough situation develops—it helps me relax and feel confident. I want to make sure you got my message. What did I say?"

   This kind of message is often a powerful one. Most of us have difficulty hearing and accepting a message like this. Because it's hard to accept, the actual message can get lost. Some of the most warm, intimate disclosures we've seen have occurred around positive shared meanings.

6. When the two of you want to "set procedures for dealing with an issue." The notion of procedure-setting will be discussed in some detail in Chapter 7. But here we want to point out that disagreements and misunderstandings about *when* to talk about something, *where* to talk about it, with *whom*, and so forth often undermine people's attempts to constructively handle issues in their relationship. Setting procedures by using the shared meaning process can be extremely helpful in facilitating constructive, rather than destructive, discussions.

7. Finally, the shared meaning process can be used to share any of the types of information found in the Awareness Wheel. Through this process both you and your partner can express your sensations, thoughts, feelings, intentions, or actions and can also find out how well you are understood. And both of you can learn what the other senses, thinks, feels, or intends, and determine how well you are understanding. And when you share Awareness Wheel

information, you will be using the skills from the first section as well as the skills specifically related to the shared meaning process.

Although most partners don't use the shared meaning process enough, it can be overused too. This usually results in stilted, over-intense dialogue:

Rachel: "How are you today?"

Aaron: "I hear you asking me about the state of my being."

Rachel: "You're right!"

Unless you're having some fun with this—mutually putting each other on—save the process for more important messages.

The key to using the shared meaning process effectively is intention—both your own and your partner's. If you want to keep some of yourself hidden from your partner and not be understood, don't initiate a shared meaning. But if, on the other hand, your intention is to send a clear and complete message and to be understood, go for shared meaning. This is particularly true if there is any doubt that message sent equals message received.

This section of the book is all about dialogue—communicating with your partner. And no matter what else happens, you just can't communicate effectively if you're not trying to understand each other. It sounds obvious, but so many partners try the impossible—continuing an attempt to communicate when there is no intention to understand. But, besides the obvious benefit of helping both of you understand the other's point of view, using the shared meaning process has other advantages. It demonstrates respect for your partner. And it shows real interest in achieving understanding, rather than manipulating or coercing your partner. These things only result, however, when both of you do have an intention to understand each other.

WHEN THE SHARED MEANING PROCESS WON'T WORK.

When the shared meaning process fails to achieve understanding, it's often because one or both of you is missing the intention to understand or to be understood. When either of you is trying to use the process to force understanding, or to try to persuade the other, it just won't work. When one of you wants to be understood but the other doesn't want to understand, there is likely to be even more misunderstanding created.

But missing intentions aren't the only reasons the shared meaning process doesn't work. Even with the best of intentions, it may not succeed because the process is easily distorted. We call these distortions "take-aways."

Receivers fall into take-aways in several ways. One is when they succumb to the urge to respond or to answer the message, rather than acknowledge it by reporting it back. If your partner sends you a message full of feelings (either positive or negative) there's an almost irresistible temptation to begin agreeing or disagreeing. But responses that begin "I agree," "That's right," "No," "I'm surprised," and a hundred others, shift the focus toward agreement or disagreement, and away from understanding.

A second take-away receivers fall into comes when they fail to speak for themselves. For example, an acknowledgement that begins, "Are you saying . . . ?" is an under-responsible statement. The receiver does not fully accept responsibility for what he hears the sender saying. Similarly, acknowledgements beginning, "You are saying . . . " are over-responsible responses. The receiver speaks for the sender by telling him what he's said. If this sounds subtle, it is. Achieving a shared meaning requires crystal clear intentions. Language is often a clue to your intentions to avoid real understanding by slipping off the mark a bit.

A third take-away is when a receiver adds new messages in his interpretation, rather than paraphrasing the original message. As we noted above, this can be difficult for the receiver to prevent, but if he tries to document his messages when he thinks he is deviating, he can minimize this kind of take-away.

Receivers aren't the only ones who can take-away. A common sender take-away after asking for shared meaning, is sending a long and complicated message as the first statement. This is a take-away because it confuses the receiver by giving him more information than he can handle. As a sender, you can prevent this from happening by keeping the initial message relatively short and simple. As a receiver starting a shared meaning, break the longer message down into smaller parts and do several shared meanings—linking shared meanings together.

Another common sender take-away occurs when the sender, in attempting to clarify his original message, changes it or adds to it. Sometimes this happens because the sender forgets what his original message was. To minimize this kind of take-away, when the sender requests a shared meaning, he should try to keep his initial message firmly in mind and stick to it until a shared meaning is reached. Then he can move on to additional messages. If, as a sender, you are not satisfied with your original message—perhaps because it was vague or confusing—indicate clearly to the receiver that you are changing the message and begin a new shared meaning.

We have some guidelines that minimize take-aways. Try to keep these in mind when you are using the shared meaning process:

Senders:

1. Be certain of the message you intend to transmit.

2. Make a brief statement, perhaps only one sentence which includes several dimensions of the Awareness Wheel.

3. Try to send the message clearly and directly.

4. Remember what you mean and how you say it.

5. Confirm your partner's accurate acknowledgement, or clarify an inaccurate one, but don't change or add to your original message.

Receivers:

1. Report back (in your own words) the message you see and hear.

2. Do not reply to the message.

3. Keep reporting back the messages you are receiving, including clarifications, until the sender confirms your accuracy.

Summary.

Communication between two people involves the exchange of information. Effective information exchange occurs when the messages sent by one person are the same as the messages received by the other. Paying close attention to the other person and using the skill of checking out go a long way toward making communication effective in our every-day lives. Furthermore, they help create good feelings in relationships by demonstrating that you care about and are interested in the other person's point of view, his thoughts, feelings, intentions, etc.

Using the shared meaning process and the associated skills can move communication even closer to being effective because it specifically focuses on accuracy. But using the shared meaning process in mundane, every-day conversations is generally inappropriate because it is time-consuming and can sound stilted. The shared meaning process, however, is very useful for insuring that understanding is achieved regarding important relationship issues. In short, the process is best used to help build relationships because it requires active participation by both partners.

CHAPTER SIX

WHAT WE TALK ABOUT

In the chapters so far, we've concentrated on two frameworks (the Awareness Wheel and shared meaning process) and a number of skills related to increasing and disclosing awareness of self and other. But in another sense, we've also been talking about the *content* of communication. We've done this in terms of the different kinds of information available in a person's own and from his partner's Awareness Wheels.

CONTENT: TYPES OF INFORMATION

We'd like to begin this chapter by presenting a transcript and showing you how a conversation proceeds when looked at in terms of the Awareness Wheel. As you read, notice how dynamic conversations are as the various kinds of information move in and out.

Dialogue	Dimension of Speaker's Awareness Wheel
Jean: "I get really *frustrated* when I have a day off or a weekend when I'm not	feeling
working / and I *want* to spend time with	intention
you. / I *want* to do something, go	intention
outside, run, ride a bike, anything. / But	
it seems you just want to sit home and	interpretation
watch television all afternoon."	

Joe: "Well, I *think* we've got a problem. / You know, I just *don't like* to get up and meet your schedule when you've got a day off to run and play through the woods. / I might *want* to do something else."	interpretation intention (preference) intention
Jean: "Well, I *interpret* that as you don't want to do it with me."	interpretation
Joe: "Now, is that what I said?"	
Jean: "No, but that's what it *looks like* to me because when I invite you to do it, you usually say, 'No, I'd rather watch TV.'"	interpretation
Joe: "Well, wouldn't you like to sit here and watch TV with me?"	
Jean: "I don't *want* to watch TV; / I get *antsy*. / When I come home and on weekends I *like* to get exercise so that I can feel good about going back to work on Monday."	intention feeling intention (preference)
Joe: "What kind of exercise are you talking about?"	
Jean: "It usually *doesn't matter*. Anything that's active. I could skate in the winter or ski or go for a walk or run or bike ride or . . . "	interpretation
Joe: "A walk *sounds* possible. / Yeah. *It's not* a matter of the time, you know, if you're talking about spending time with me, there are different ways we can spend time with each other and maybe different times that we can spend away from each other. / Do you want to spend the whole weekend with me? I mean I've got some other things I *want* to do too. I've got some things for school, I've got a	interpretation interpretation intention

paper due for American Studies. So
there are a lot of those things that are
happening with me too. / But *let me try*
to tell you what I think I'm hearing you
say."

action

Jean: "I *don't think* you understand
what I'm saying."

interpretation

Joe: "Okay, well, let me see if I *can*
identify. / I *heard* you say you like to do
things active when you've got some
time and you get antsy sitting around
here and you get frustrated when I don't
want to get up and get going at the crack
of dawn, which is one of the things you
like to do. / And you know me, man, I
like to sleep."

action
sensing

intention (preference)

Jean: "Yeah, *you've* got it. / But how
would you *feel* if I did that?

interpretation
feeling

Joe: "Fine, I like you to go out and
exercise; you can exercise for me."

Jean: "I *enjoy* doing it by myself, / but I
don't *want* you to feel bad and think that
I don't want you along. / And yet when
you don't do it I *wonder* whether we're
this together family 'cause we don't do
stuff together."

feeling
intention

interpretation

Joe: "I don't *know* where you're getting
that because you know . . . / One of the
things that I *like* doing with you is doing
things where we can go someplace and
talk, and sometimes we can talk while
we walk, but I don't like jogging . . .
And skiing you know, I could maybe
think of cross country skiing but getting
up early to go downhill skiing or
something like that is not where it's at."

interpretation

intention (preference)

Jean: "But you're *not* saying that you
don't want me to do it."

interpretation

Joe: "NO. I *want* you to because I think that's something you enjoy, it's obvious . . . "

— intention

Jean: "That's really hard for me to *believe* that you really want me to do it but I *believe* you. / Because *last Friday* when I did it and came back, I was really excited and *saw* you smiling and you seemed to get some excitement from my enjoyment. / And *it seemed* like it was better the rest of the day / even though you watch TV, I *watch* you watching TV, and / I felt better because I did my own thing."

— action*
— sensing
    (documenting)

— interpretation

— action
— feeling

Joe: "Yeah, when I *watch* TV I'm doin' my own thing."

— action

Jean: "I know. But it's really hard for me *to think* that everybody doesn't want to exercise as I do."

— action*

*Words which report the speaker's active cognitive action (e.g., thinking, assuming, trusting, believing—being verbs) are included as action statements.

This conversation can be described as involving a pretty good mixture of the different kinds of information identified in the Awareness Wheel. Here the conversation is pictured in the form of a pie representing each dimension of the Awareness Wheel.

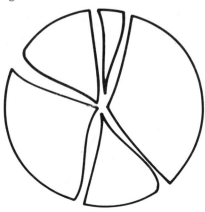

Other conversations frequently have rather imbalanced forms. For example, many every day chit-chats are friendly reports of sensations, thoughts and actions:

> "I saw Mary in class today and she said she'll have her paper finished by the end of the week."

> "I've been thinking about taking some tennis lessons."

> "I stopped at the store and picked up some bread and milk on the way home."

Occasionally, feelings and intentions are mentioned. They add flavor and orientation to the conversations.

In heated arguments, lots of interpretation and action statements are made. They usually are about the other person:

> Mel: "You sure bore people when you tell one of your ten minute stories" (evaluation of other's behavior).

> Sue: "I didn't dominate the conversation; everyone talked a lot" (self-evaluation of action, defending against other's evaluation).

> Mel: "Well, you should watch it" (prescription for other's future action).

Although both partners have lots of feelings and intentions during the heat of the argument, these are not being disclosed directly.

Now try to think about some of the conversations you have had with your partner in terms of the Awareness Wheel. Do one or two kinds of information usually dominate? Do different types of conversations, such as, making a plan, relaxing and sharing events of the day, arguing, etc., form different pies? How do the pies differ? If your conversations almost always leave out one or two dimensions, you and your partner may be operating out of limited awareness. Looking at your conversations in this way may help you find out what these limitations might be.

CONTENT: THE FOCUS OF CONVERSATION

A second way of discussing content is in terms of what your

conversation is about—what the *focus* is. As we observe conversations in terms of the Awareness Wheel, we look at the dimensions of awareness being disclosed—sensations, thoughts, feelings, intentions, or actions. When we observe conversations in terms of focus, we emphasize the things, events, or persons *being referred to* or talked about. We distinguish *five* different foci of messages—topic, self, partner, relationship, and mixed.

A *topic-message* focuses on things, events, ideas, places or people who are not immediately present. Topic-messages include all statements that are not directly about you, your partner, or the two of you together. Anything except me, you, or us. People become a topic when they're not immediately present and you talk about them (e.g., kids, friends, parents, boss, etc.).

"The kids have sure been restless today."

"Your mother called and said she's planning to visit us next month."

"What time does the bank open?"

"The party last night was fun.',

"Is there gas in the car?"

"Boy, was Bill mad about getting a 'C' in that course!"

"John was sure trying to make Beth believe he's naive."

All of these statements refer to events or persons outside the present situation.

A message focusing on *self* talks about you as a person, about your experiences, thoughts, feelings, etc.

"I usually feel confident."

"I've had a hard time concentrating lately."

"I'm not sure what I want to do."

"I'll be ready to go in a minute."

All of these statements report on some experience the speaker has had, is having, or anticipates having. Self-messages express the speaker's thoughts or interpretations, as well as his feelings, intentions, or actions. Generally, conversations about self are likely to include more dimensions of the Awareness Wheel than topic conversations.

The same is true of conversations about your partner, his experiences, thoughts, and feelings. *Partner-messages* are pretty similar to self-messages, although they may involve more interpretations than self-messages:

> "What will happen if you don't hear by Wednesday?"

> "You really seem worried about that."

> "Do you expect to finish today?"

> "I think you can do it. You've done it before."

> "How do you feel?"

Both self-messages and partner-messages focus on a single person, either me or you. In this sense, their focus is personal. Because these messages are about either me or you, they express more personal involvement than topic-messages. Another kind of message also has a great deal of personal involvement: a *relationship-message*.

When you or your partner say something about the two of you together—you *and* me—you are expressing relationship messages. Relationship messages report the awareness you have *in relation to* your partner, and vice versa:

> "I really feel pleased when you listen to me carefully."

> "I think we spend too much time analysing our relationship— sometimes this keeps me from being spontaneous with you."

> "I'd like to study with you tonight, but I'm concerned that we won't get enough work done. I'm really flooded right now."

> "I love you."

As a rule, relationship-messages demonstrate or show evidence of relationship. This is done by talking about you and me, my thoughts-your feelings, your actions-my intentions, etc.

Relationship-messages get sticky when you make assumptions about both of you together and don't speak for yourself:

"We sure had a good time last night"—(maybe your partner did, maybe s/he didn't).

"It's okay that you do all the deciding for me."

"We both see it that way, don't we?"

"That always happens to us."

"Our feelings are the same because we are so close."

These kinds of messages fail to appreciate that each partner may experience things differently.

Just like conversations about self or partner, conversations about your relationship are likely to include more dimensions of the Awareness Wheel than topic conversations. In fact, relationship-messages seem to be more likely to include feelings and intentions than either self or partner-messages.

We call the last type of focus, mixed. Here topic messages are mixed with self, partner, or relationship messages. Most conversations tend to be mixed unless the speaker is focusing specifically on self, partner or the two of them in relationship to each other:

"I don't know if Ted saw me." (Self-Topic)

"What kind of car do you like best?" (Partner-Topic)

"I like the way you can get involved with the kids." (Relationship-Topic)

Now we'd like you to read the same transcript you read before, but this time look at it in terms of the focus of the statements. Again, as you read, notice how the focus shifts from relationship to self to partner, to topic, and back to relationship, etc., even within a single sentence. We think the transcript will show you how dynamic conversations are in terms of focus, as well as the kinds of information expressed. (When the focus is mixed with topic, we've marked this with an asterisk.)

Dialogue	Focus
Jean: "I get really frustrated when I have a day off or a weekend when I'm not working and I want to spend time with you. / I want to do something, go outside, run, ride a bike, anything. / But it seems you just want to sit home and watch television all afternoon."	relationship self* (activities) partner* (TV)
Joe: "Well, I think we've got a problem. You know, I just don't like to get up and meet your schedule when you've got a day off to run and play through the woods. / I might want to do something else."	relationship* (schedules) self
Jean: "Well, I interpret that as you don't want to do it with me."	relationship
Joe: "Now, is that what I said?"	self
Jean: "No, but that's what it looks like to me because when I invite you to do it, you usually say, 'No I'd rather watch TV.'"	relationship* (TV)
Joe: "Well, wouldn't you like to sit here and watch TV with me?"	relationship* (TV)
Jean: "I don't want to watch TV; I get antsy. When I come home and on weekends I like to get exercise so that I can feel good about going back to work on Monday."	self* (TV, exercise)
Joe: "What kind of exercise are you talking about?"	partner* (exercise)
Jean: "It usually doesn't matter. Anything that's active. I could skate in the winter or ski or go for a walk or run or bike ride or . . ."	self* (activities)

*indicates mixed focus

Joe: "A walk sounds possible. Yeah. / It's not a matter of the time, you know, if you're talking about spending time with me, there are different ways we can spend time with each other and maybe different times that we can spend away from each other. / Do you want to spend the whole weekend with me? / I mean I've got some other things I want to do, too. I've got some things for school, I've got a paper due for American Studies. So there are a lot of those things that are happening with me too. / But let me try to tell you what I think I'm hearing you say."	topic relationship* (ways) relationship self* (things to do) relationship
Jean: "I don't think you understand what I'm saying."	relationship
Joe: "Okay, well let me see if I can identify. / I heard you say you like to do things active when you've got some time and you get antsy sitting around here and you get frustrated when I don't want to get up and get going at the crack of dawn, which is one of the things you like to do. / And you know me, man, I like to sleep."	self relationship* (activities) self* (sleep)
Jean: Yeah, you've got it. / But how would you feel if I did that?"	partner relationship
Joe: "Fine, I like you to go out and exercise; you can exercise for me."	relationship* (exercise)
Jean: "I enjoy doing it by myself, but I don't want you to feel bad and think that I don't want you along. / And yet when you don't do it I wonder whether we're this together family 'cause we don't do stuff together."	relationship relationship

Joe: "I don't know where you're getting   relationship*
that because you know . . . One of the   (activities)
things that I like doing with you is doing
things where we can go someplace and
talk, and sometimes we can talk while
we walk, but I don't like jogging . . . /
And skiing you know, I could maybe   self* (skiing)
think of cross country skiing but getting
up early to go downhill skiing or
something like that is not where it's at."

Jean: "But you're not saying that you   partner
don't want me to do it."

Joe: "NO. I want you to because I think   relationship
that's something you enjoy, it's obvious
. . . "

Jean: "That's really hard for me to   relationship
believe that you really want me to do it
but I believe you. Because last Friday
when I did it and came back, I was really
excited and saw you smiling and you
seemed to get some excitement from my
enjoyment. / And it seemed like it was   relationship* (TV)
better the rest of the day even though
you watch TV, I watch you watching
TV, and I felt better because I did my
own thing."

Joe: "Yeah, when I watch TV I'm doin'   self* (TV)
my own thing."

Jean: "I know. But it's really hard for me   self* (exercise)
to think that everybody doesn't want to
exercise as I do."

    This conversation can be described in the form of a square. Each
category is represented. The inner part represents self, partner, and
relationship mixed with topic:

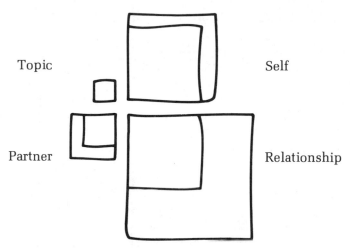

Topic

Self

Partner

Relationship

Just as conversations take a lot of different shapes when looked at in terms of the Awareness Wheel, so do they when viewed in terms of focus. Chit-chats are heavily topic-focused with self-messages entering when a person tells an anecdote or story about himself. Arguments involve many partner-messages with accusations or evaluations of partner's actions. Also during arguments, many self-messages tend to be denials, e.g., "I'm not that way," or "I don't do that very often." But distinguishing "chit-chat" and "arguments" gets us into styles of communication, and that's what Section III is all about.

We'd like you to stop a moment again and try to think of some of the conversations you have had with your partner in terms of *focus*. Are your conversations heavily topic-focused, or do a substantial number of self, partner, and relationship messages occur, too. When do your conversations include the more person-centered messages? When you're arguing? When you're sharing feelings? When you're making a decision? If your conversations are almost entirely topic-focused, you're probably keeping a lot of life out of your relationship. This is because relationships come alive only when you and your partner get involved with each other, and that's almost impossible unless your conversations focus very frequently on self, partner, or the two of you together.

We've been talking about the *focus* of your messages, separately from the kind of information (sensations, thoughts, feelings, etc.)

included in these messages. But they aren't separate, of course. Actually, if you begin to focus on self in your messages, you begin disclosing your awareness. The same thing can happen if you focus on your contribution to your relationship and speak for self. If you talk about your response to your partner, you will naturally be talking about your relationship and sharing your self-awareness. Or, approaching it from the other direction, if you begin sharing your feelings and intentions with your partner, your focus is likely to shift from topic to self to your relationship.

One caution—prolonged focus on your partner, without your partner's invitation to do so, usually suggests you're not in contact with your own self-awareness and your own contributions/ response to your relationship with your partner. In the short run, maybe people find it easier to talk about topics or their partner (usually with a hidden agenda to get him to change) rather than stay in contact with their own immediate experience. Focusing on topics or partner often has the effect of holding events and other people, not yourself, responsible for what's happening to you.

TOPIC, PERSONAL, AND RELATIONSHIP ISSUES

We have been discussing the focus of messages and conversations to increase your awareness and choice of what to talk about. We think you'll be able to send clearer messages when you can recognize your own communication behavior; for example, recognizing limited disclosures versus complete disclosure of your awareness; or identifying conversations limited to one focus versus many.

Knowing something about the difference between topic, personal (self or partner) and relationship messages has another very important function. A context is provided for understanding different types of issues which are important to your continued personal and partnership growth and development. Different issues correspond with different foci.

What's meant by the term "issue?" We will be using the word frequently and our definition is as follows: An issue may be *anything which concerns one or both partners, implies choice, and has implications for personal and/or relationship growth.* What is important about this definition is that each person in the partnership is his own authority on his experience. Something doesn't have to be of concern to both partners in order for it to be an issue. If I'm excited or upset about something, it's an issue for me. Whether I disclose this concern to my partner is my choice. If I do share it with my partner, s/he in turn can acknowledge my concern, identify it as only my concern or his/her concern as well, and deal with the issue—or choose to ignore it. Finally, an issue has implications for at least one if not both partners concerned, because it involves someone's Awareness Wheel.

An issue exists when there is something incomplete or incongruent. The issue exists until there is some individual or partnership resolution. In short, an issue is old or new unfinished business.

Everyone has issues of concern in his daily life. At different points in time, different issues come in and out of focus. For example, if my partner and I are comfortably settled in an apartment, we have no issue regarding our residence. But any number of things can change this and raise new issues—a decision to have a baby, a promotion opportunity in a different community, need for a place to study if one of us returns to school. And when something like this happens—when new options enter our relationship—a new set of issues emerge, such as where we're going to live, or how we're going to move, and perhaps more important, how we're going to make decisions about these things.

Issues are not the same as problems. Issues are a part of life; they're the difference between what is being done and what sometimes must be done, between what isn't and what is wanted. Issues can be recurrent, such as spending decisions. Even if an issue is a recurrent one, it does not have to become a problem. An issue becomes a problem, however, when it is recurrent *and* the decisions you and your partner make (or fail to make) are consistently unsatisfactory to one or both of you.

To help you get a better handle on some of the issues most partners have to deal with at one time or another, we've grouped a number of them under the three categories—topic, personal, relationship.

Figure 6-1   Different Types of Issues

Topic

housing	leisure	transportation
friends	contraception	drugs
career	education	pets
relatives	time	moving
children	space	housekeeping
money	clothes/goods	food

Personal

self-esteem	communication skills	achievement
identity	body/image	success
values	expectations	failure
freedom	faith	appearance
recognition	habits	goals
energy	health	creativity
responsibility	aloneness	

Relationship

mutuality/autonomy	celebration
togetherness/apartness	sex
closeness/distance	trust
privacy/company	jealousy
equality/precedence	affection
stability/instability	commitment
agreement/disagreement	decision-making
similarity/difference	rules
communication patterns	boundaries
understanding/misunderstanding	inclusion/exclusion
cooperation/competition	control

As you look over the list, which of them are important to you at the present time, individually and with your partner? Can you identify some that you are currently dealing with and others which you find yourself avoiding? Can you locate some which have been important in the past as well as some that you anticipate in the future? Perhaps you can identify some concerns that are important to you but do not appear on this list.

Thinking again about the dialogue between Jean and Joe at the beginning of this chapter, what were the issues there? At the topic level, they were discussing leisure (recreation), and timing (schedules). At the personal level they were expressing differences in energy and values. At the relationship level, they were dealing with mutuality and autonomy—togetherness and apartness.

There are a number of different issues common to all of us. Likewise, there are many different ways of dealing with these issues—constructing some kind of a complete, congruent and comfortable balance with them. The variety of outcomes or solutions to situations created by these issues is infinite. Because of this, we're not interested in offering solutions in this book. We are interested in increasing your *awareness*, *skills*, and *choice* around the process of how you approach and resolve issues.

The Relationship Among Issues.

We will be saying more about the role of issues in the following chapters. But before leaving this section on focus, we want to say a bit more about the relationship among topic, personal and relationship issues.

Figure 6-2   The Relationship Among Issues

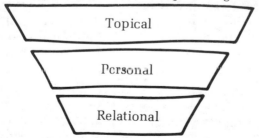

Figure 6-2 presents a diagram of the relationship among these three clusters. Topic issues are located at the top to represent a broad spectrum of issues which relate you, as a person, to the world around you. We've located personal issues in the middle to suggest a deeper set of issues which serve as a focal point, interfacing both topic concerns and relationship bonds. Finally, we locate relationship issues at a lower and deeper level. Intimacy and risk generally increase as you move down from topic to person to relationship issues. The risk is that the more I disclose about myself, the less control I have over how you will respond to what I say.

Although we're making some distinctions in terms of levels of issues, we do not mean to imply that each level is not important in its own time and place. Conversations limited mainly to topics can be bland, while dialogue limited largely to relationships can become too heavy and solemn. Again, all kinds of issues are important but they differ in their intensity. The point here is that some partners are not able to deal with the full spectrum of issues. Rather, for one reason or another, they are limited in their awareness, comfort and skill in meeting and dealing with them.

As you looked at the diagram in Figure 6-2, perhaps you realized that it is possible to confuse your communication with your partner by talking about an issue at one level (topical for example) while your primary experience is really at a personal or relationship level. For example, it's quite common for couples to hassle each other about money when, in fact, their conflict is really at a relationship level, e.g., a struggle for control. As another example, energy can be centered on disciplining of the children (a topical issue) when incongruent personal values and unresolved relational consensus about similarity and difference go unattended. We don't intend to imply by these examples that all topical issues really involve deeper concerns. But we do suggest that you tune into your Awareness Wheel very carefully to find the most significant level of your personal concern. It may be at a different level than the one you are focusing on.

A second way communication can become confused is by changing issues abruptly during the discussion. For example, one of the authors recalls a student who was talking about how hard it was for her to acknowledge her own feelings; suddenly she shifted and began to blame her mother for how she was raised. In effect, by changing the focus from herself to her mother she gave up responsibility for her immediate experience and shifted her focus. This is very easy to do, with or without awareness. The focus of communication may change for many reasons, but common ones include the following: when an issue is no longer alive; when an issue gets too close for comfort; when there is new and legitimate information to introduce; or when a person wants to avoid an issue. Again, it all depends on your intention.

Maintaining focus on an issue, staying in contact with your own awareness, and supporting your partner's awareness, is often difficult. In this chapter we've tried to clarify the various things you can talk about in your conversations with other people—the focus of your message. We've also tried to interrelate this with your Awareness Wheel and with levels of issues which are important to you and your partner. We think knowing something about these differences can help you identify what you want to talk about—the things that are important to you—when you want to. And we think it can help you identify your own issues and begin to move toward solutions best for you.

CHAPTER SEVEN

UNDERSTANDING/MISUNDERSTANDING; AGREEMENT/DIFFERENCE

1. How often do you *know* what your partner thinks, feels, wants?
2. How often are you sure that your partner understands what you're thinking, feeling, and wanting?
3. How often do you discover that you've misunderstood each other?
4. How often has misunderstanding created difficulties for the two of you?
5. How often do you experience joy, realizing your partner understands what you're experiencing?

UNDERSTANDING/MISUNDERSTANDING

The loneliest people in the world are usually people who are frequently misunderstood. To be stuck with thoughts, feelings, and intentions that no one else really knows about is an awful place to be stuck. We feel connected with someone else when we're understood, and rightly so because this usually means someone cares enough about us to understand us. Besides the good feelings that come from being understood, understanding is an important ingredient in keeping relationships alive. When you and your partner understand one another, you enhance your capacity for mutuality in your relationship. When you understand one another, you have a good idea of what to expect from each other. And this creates a certain degree of predictability which is invaluable for deepening your relationship.

Imagine what it would be like to never know what to expect from your partner, or if your partner never knew what to expect from you. In this case, total uncertainty would be predictable! Typically this is an anxiety-producing state which is not very conducive to relationship building.

Some interesting research compared twelve troubled marriages with twelve non-troubled marriages.[1] The researchers found that couples in the troubled relationships more often misunderstood one another and more often felt misunderstood. And further, these partners were less able to correctly identify the specific issue on which misunderstanding existed!

This research shows pretty clearly that misunderstanding is at least a strong symptom of relationship problems, if not a cause. Many difficulties are generated by misunderstanding, and feelings of disappointment, anger, and loneliness are associated with chronic misunderstanding. Nevertheless, it is probably impossible for partners to avoid having some misunderstanding in their relationship. That's because a lot of effort is involved in the understanding process, as we have seen in Chapter 5.

The impact of misunderstanding on a relationship depends partly on how frequently it occurs. But it also depends on what the misunderstanding is about. If a misunderstanding occurs concerning a topic such as your partner's political preferences or impressions of a neighbor, the impact is not likely to be very significant. But as the misunderstanding involves you or your

[1]Laing, R.D., H Phillipson, and A.R. Lee, Interpersonal Perception: A Theory and Method of Research, New York: Springer, 1966.

partner as a person or your relationship, the impact becomes increasingly significant.

Sources of Misunderstanding.

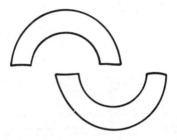

"A form of cruelty in human interaction is to deliberately misunderstand the other. It is not simply misunderstanding however; rather, it is misunderstanding based on understanding . . . A nasty fight is one in which the other deliberately misconstrues what you are saying. He acts in a manner that says you are not coming through at all the way you think you are.[1]

It is possible that you or your partner deliberately misunderstand. But intentional misunderstanding is not typical between partners. Two other reasons for misunderstanding are much more common.

Reason 1: "Failure to Disclose Information, or Failure to Encourage Disclosure."

When your partner does not have access to your Awareness Wheel, the information you have about yourself, then you increase the chances of being misunderstood. And when you don't encourage disclosure from your partner, it's likely you're going to misunderstand him. Remember: understanding is a process with mutual responsibility for disclosing information and encouraging disclosure. Too often only limited awareness is expressed. With limited awareness and partial disclosure, each of you may

[1] Joseph Luft. *Of Human Interaction* (Palo Alto, Calif.: National Press Books, 1969), pp. 143-44.

understand some things about the other, but not enough. For example:

> Jim noticed that Cathy seemed angry, (abrupt movements, slamming door, frowning) and he assumed that Cathy was angry with him, for one of several possible reasons. Jim began to feel angry toward Cathy and spoke coldly and brusquely to her. This precipitated a flare-up. Actually, Cathy was angry about something that had nothing to do with Jim. She was unaware of the impact of her behavior on Jim, and Jim failed to check out his assumption about the meaning of Cathy's behavior.

When only partial understanding occurs, partners often make guesses about things going on inside the other. They also act on assumptions they have not checked out. By guessing and assuming they try to fill in their partner's Awareness Wheel.

Unfortunately, the folklore about close relationships (especially marriage) encourages couples to act on the basis of unchecked assumptions: "If a couple is really close, each will know what the other thinks, feels, and wants without a word being spoken." There's just enough truth to this to perpetuate the myth, i.e., people who know each other really well over a long period become better guessers, better able to read signals and anticipate each other. But a guess is still a guess, and several television shows have become popular by revealing how often married couples are mistaken about each other's inner workings. We've noticed that for some people the mark of a good relationship is when you know each other so well that you don't have to ask. But for us, the mark of a good relationship is that when you want something you feel free to ask, secure in the knowledge that your wants will be respected, even if not necessarily agreed to or provided for. An alternative to guessing and assuming is using the Awareness Wheel to help each other increase understanding:

> Jean: "It bothers me that I say what I don't like about you much more often than you do about me. I wish you'd speak up more."
>
> Rob: "Do you think you're being demanding?"

Jean: "Well, it's not that so much as I wish you'd more often let me know what's going on inside of you. It seems to me I tell you directly when I don't like something you do, but I think it's sort of one-sided. I sometimes notice you becoming quiet and unhappy-looking, and I'm pretty sure it's about something I've done or said, but you don't really tell me what it's about."

Rob: "You'd rather I came right out with it? Yeah. But I think you might get sore."

Jean: "Sure, I might. But I'd still much rather you told me directly what it's about. I'd rather get mad than have a feeling of coldness and distance between us."

Rob: "I didn't realize my silence comes across as coldness and distance. I thought I was just being very patient."

Jean: "That's not what I want from you. I'd rather you tell me what's going on."

Reason 2: "Assuming That Once Something Has Been Said, It's Been Understood."

The idea that now that it's been said, now that the words are on the table, my partner is sure to understand. Lots of luck! This basic error in communication comes from the assumption that meanings are in words. But are they? Look at this:

Rick: "You really look cute in that outfit."

Sue: "Cute! What's so 'cute' about it?"

Rick: "Hey, why're you sore? I paid you a compliment."

Sue: "I don't think it's a compliment."

OR

Laura: "I'd like us to develop more openness in our relationship."

Jerry: "Well, if I'm not open enough for you, you can just forget about it."

Laura: "Hey, wait a minute! I don't think you understood what I meant by 'openness'."

These people are probably viewing the words "cute" and "openness" in different ways. But meanings are inside you; they are not in the words you use. Saying that meanings are in people, rather than in words, isn't meant to imply that every one has totally different meanings for the same words. If that were so, communication would be impossible. Actually, most people share roughly the same meaning for most words. This is true in part because of the context in which things are said. But it's the subtle differences that get us into trouble. "Roughly sharing" the same meaning is "roughly understanding" one another. In intimate partnerships, rough understanding on important issues usually doesn't do the job.

Dropping the assumption that meanings are in words and adopting the view that they are in people is more important than you may imagine. The two views carry a number of implications for how communication occurs and how you can communicate effectively. Listed below are some of these implications:

If meanings are in words then:	If meanings are in people then:
1. Given a common vocabulary, the message means the same for both sender and receiver.	1. Sender and receiver will frequently not have exactly the same meaning for the message, even if they share the same words.
2. The major responsibility for success lies with the receiver in his decoding of the sender's words.	2. The major responsibility for success lies with both the sender and receiver. Communication consists of transactions between two communicators— matching message sent with message received.

3. If errors occur, the major reason usually lies with the receiver; once in a while it might be the sender if he uses the wrong words.

3. If error occurs, the major reason is in the transaction between communicators.

4. Acknowledgement (feedback) is not important.

4. Feedback is essential.

5. Most of the available time and energy goes into the construction of a correct message.

5. Time and energy are divided among the initial message, acknowledgement, and encoding additional messages.

6. Communication breakdown justifies blame.

6. Communication breakdown can be altered by increased awareness.

7. When there are differences, one person's right, the other's wrong.

7. There are several ways to look at the same situation.

Do you see the difference? It's almost as though two different languages are being spoken. They involve two different sets of assumptions and processes. Understanding (sharing meaning) doesn't often happen if the two of you see the world from these two very different perspectives. If you keep this difference in mind, some misunderstanding and unnecessary conflict can be reduced.

The point we want to stress is this. We hope you don't automatically assume that:

1. just because you've said it, your partner understands it;

2. just because you've heard your partner, you understand him.

We hope you keep alert to the possibility that misunderstanding can still occur, and if you think it is happening, take action. Pull out the Awareness Wheel at times like that and check it out. Use it to pay close attention to your partner's message. Use it to ask yourself and your partner, what's meant, felt, or intended. Or share a meaning.

AGREEMENT/DISAGREEMENT

Many people view disagreement as a sign that there is something "wrong" in the relationship, i.e., "you should think, feel, and act as I do. If you don't, you don't love me."[1]

We think this view tends to cloud what are actually three separate issues:

1. What is the optimal balance between stability and instability in your relationship?

2. What is the optimal balance between agreement and disagreement in your relationship?

3. What is the optimal balance between sameness and difference in your relationship?

Let's look at some of the differences between these issues.

The issue of stability-instability refers to the kinds of patterns a partnership uses in making decisions, communicating, and so forth. Highly stable ones tend to use only one or two patterns across a wide variety of issues and topics, whereas highly unstable partnerships tend to have a near absence of patterns, varying radically even when dealing with the same kind of issue or topic. Thus, highly stable systems are very predictable, and highly unstable systems are quite unpredictable.

[1]Virginia Satir, *Peoplemaking* (Palo Alto, Calif.: Science and Behavior Books, 1972), p. 137.

The issue of agreement-disagreement refers to partner's values, attitudes, opinions, and the like. High agreement relationships are those in which both partners agree on almost every topic and have nearly identical values. High disagreement relationships are just the opposite with little agreement on any topic or value.

The issue of sameness-differentness refers to partner's behaviors, experiences, and information. In relationships with high sameness, both partners are very similar in their behavior—how they do things, what their experiences have been, and in the kinds of information they have. Relationships high in differences are those whose partners have widely diverging behaviors, experiences, and information.

These separate issues tend to become clouded because they have similar impacts on relationships. When there is an extremely high degree of stability, agreement, or sameness in a relationship, the relationship tends to be rather bland and perhaps boring. The partners can only supplement each other's viewpoints and behaviors, rather than complementing one another with a variety of perspectives and behaviors. When new information is presented to the system or when new issues emerge, the system responds from a limited, unitary viewpoint and fails to engage in a "point-counterpoint" or "thesis-antithesis" dialogue in the process of resolving the issue.

On the other hand, when there is an extremely high degree of instability, disagreement, or differentness, the relationship tends to be an uncertain one. High amounts of energy are spent in dealing with tension and conflict. There are too few occasions when partners experience the satisfaction of being "together." New information and new issues typically result in increased anxiety, not in personal or relationship growth.

Most relationships don't operate at either of these two extremes, of course, but some do. When this happens, unfortunate consequences for the relationship may result. It seems to be the case that some balance is necessary between these two extremes for any relationship, if personal and relationship growth is to occur.

There is *no precise formula* to indicate what kind of balance a relationship should have on each of these dimensions. But, Satir has captured the essential notion of the necessity of such a balance very succinctly:[1]

> "Two people are first interested in each other because of their sameness, but they remain interested over the years because of their differences. If humans never find their sameness, they will never meet; if they never meet their differentness, they cannot be real or develop a truly human and zestful relationship with one another."

As you continue to read in this section, we'd like you to keep two things in mind. First, if one or both partners in a relationship strive to maintain perfect stability, agreement, and sameness, this effort can exact a high price, robbing potential personal and relationship growth. Second, disagreements and differences as well as new information and new issues are bound to occur, because even the most similar partners are not identical and have different experiences, contacts, etc. When differences or disagreements arise or when new things happen in a relationship, there is a significant opportunity for personal and relationship development. Typically these things create a potential for change, and they can be used constructively to move your relationship in directions you choose if they are dealt with directly.

Now let's look at a transcript of a couple dealing directly with an important issue. As you read, pay attention to the various levels of topic, personal, and relationship issues that come into focus. And notice the potential areas for increased personal and relationship growth.

> Amy: "You know we've been sitting with the checkbook noticing the needs of the kids increasing financially—and now college is coming up. I guess the question on my mind is what are the possibilities of me going to work and if I do, what are going to be the effects on both of us. I'd like to spend some time talking about this."
>
> Don: "Well, I'd like to do that, too. I'd just as soon talk about it now. How about you?"

[1]Virginia Satir, *Peoplemaking* (Palo Alto, Calif.: Science Behavior Books, 1972), p. 138.

Amy: "Yeah, I would too. But I'm a bit concerned we may not have enough time."

Don: "Maybe we won't, but we can pick up on it again another night. I'd want to do that. All right?"

Amy: "Okay. I'm wondering, I don't have any particular job in mind so we're going to have to do a little speculating as far as, you know, if I got this kind of job it would possibly offer this kind of income and what would that do to our total income. So it's going to be difficult right now to be specific. I just want to air some things that I am thinking and feeling."

Don: "Okay."

Amy: "Well, I have mixed feelings, and this is what I don't know—which feelings are the strongest. I suppose if I had my druthers I'm most comfortable at home, but I also know that I enjoy being around people so I think I could enjoy myself working outside the home. I would have to make some decisions I think as to what I would give up as far as my other activities and this is going to be tough for me."

Don: "So the thought of going to work is kind of a mixed bag for you."

Amy: "Yeah, it is. I would do it first of all because of the money. I also think I could and would enjoy it. At least, partly. I wouldn't enjoy clerking at Kresge's, I wouldn't do that. I wouldn't get enjoyment out of that. There is one particular job opportunity that's open right now. I have no idea if I would get it. I want to look into it. What I'm wondering is what will an income increase of this much do to our income tax. Will it be financially of benefit for me to earn that much or will that much just put us in this next income bracket and make our income tax go up so we haven't gained anything by that."

Don: "Well, we can estimate that quite accurately once we know the amount. Because right now we could take 22 and be pretty close to what the income tax addition would be. So if $22 of every $100 that you earn would be income tax, so that leaves you with $78.

Amy: "Out of a hundred."

Don: "Right. And I think that is an issue. I think that's one consideration that we have to look at. I have some feelings about your going to work. I have in the past kept you from really thinking about going to work partly because I thought that it was very important for you to be at home with our five children and all of their needs and coming home at noon, noon lunches and many things. I guess you'd say that's the old fashioned idea that mothers should be home with the kids. I felt very comfortable about that. Now I see a change coming in terms of the styles of families, and I don't feel uncomfortable with your going to work. In fact I feel kind of excited by it. Not just for the dollar income. In fact, I would hope that isn't the major motivation, although it certainly is important.

Notice how smoothly Don and Amy shift foci beginning with a topic (Amy's consideration of going to work), setting procedures, then moving to a personal focus (Amy's feelings and intentions about a job), back to a topic (the income question), then on to a personal focus (Don's feelings about the idea of Amy's working). In reading the transcript, one gets the impression that the focus shifts are natural as this couple begins to define and identify the major issues of concern.

All of this happened because of the introduction of new information into the relationship—Amy's indication that she is considering going to work. What are the outcomes from this brief segment? First, as the conversation proceeds, it appears that Amy's awareness of her intentions becomes clearer. Initially, she acknowledges that she has some conflict, but then begins to spell out different goals she would have in working. Second, Don's self-awareness appears to increase, too. In his last statement, Don appears almost to be thinking out loud as he reflects on a change in his view of Amy's working. Third, they begin to clear the way for dealing with various relationship issues that may be involved in Amy's working (e.g., togetherness/apartness, equality/complementarity, boundaries) by starting to sort out some of the topic and personal issues also involved in this kind of decision.

In short, Amy and Don have effectively used new information to open new possibilities for each of them. And it took only a few minutes to set this process in motion. Two things seem tò happen and make this possible. First, both Amy and Don dealt with the issue directly and openly with high disclosure. In particular, both stated their feelings and intentions. Second, both seemed to try to gain an understanding of the other's point of view, using checking out and shared meaning, before closing down on the issue. Instead of identifying an issue quickly and proposing a rapid solution, they took the time to identify the several related issues involved and to share an understanding of these issues. In fact, in this dialogue, they did not even begin to consider solutions. We think both of these processes are important if issues are to serve as growth points—complete and direct personal disclosure and striving for understanding before decision.

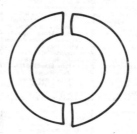

As we close this section on Agreement/Disagreement, we call your attention to an area where agreement is necessary, i.e., agreement about procedures for dealing with an issue. Early in their discussion, Don and Amy reached agreement about *what* they would talk about, *when,* and for *how long*. Their agreement on these procedural matters was an essential feature in the productiveness of their discussion. In the next section, we will focus on various aspects of procedure setting.

RELATIONSHIP RULES: ANOTHER LEVEL OF ISSUES

The kinds of issues we have been talking about occur in every relationship. And whether you are aware of it or not, every relationship you have is governed to a certain extent by a set of informal rules. These are called "Rules of Relationship."[1] One way to get a handle on these rules is to think in terms of *who* can do

[1]Watzlawick, P., J. H. Beavin, and D. D. Jackson, *The Pragmatics of Human Communication.* New York: Norton, 1967.

what, where, when, and *how?* All of your relationships, with parents, friends, lover, children, employer, teachers, and acquaintances have their own sets of unique rules. So, for instance, depending on the intimacy and nature of the relationship, what you can talk about with whom, when, where and how varies considerably.

Another way of looking at rules is to think in terms of whom you can share your awareness with completely and congruently. Are you comfortable doing this with your parents, certain friends, children, employer, or other associates? In some relationships, complete disclosure is encouraged and enjoyed. In others, informal rules exist which say complete disclosure is off-limits. In these, perhaps you can talk about your thoughts and actions but don't get into what you feel and want. When you enter the forbidden, you're breaking a rule of your relationship and tension usually arises. No one will say, "Hey, you can't talk about that." But oftentimes the conversation falls silent, a comment is ignored, there's a change in focus, or an argument erupts.

Pause for a moment, think about the different things you can and cannot talk about with different people you know. Do you find differences between what you can talk about with your parents, brothers, and sisters? How does this compare with what you can disclose to your partner? How does this compare to how comfortable you are relating to certain teachers, business associates, friends of the opposite sex, or the same sex? Finally, how do others in these different relationships let you know when you've broken an unwritten and unspoken rule between the two of you?

In several respects, the rules in a relationship operate like the rules of a game. Rules do a lot to make any game unique. Similarly, a large part of the uniqueness of each relationship is the particular rules of the specific relationship. Further, rules in a game are essential for providing meaningful and satisfactory play. The same is true of relationships. And when the participants in a relationship constantly change the rules, chaos occurs. The exact same thing happens when the rules of a game are arbitrarily changed. The result of this chaos in relationships—and in games—typically is ineffectiveness and dissatisfaction for the partners. In short, rules underlie certain expectations and help define boundaries and activities which facilitate predictability and trust in a relationship.

In many instances, how you and your partner go about dealing with issues in your relationship reflects the unwritten rules of your relationship—who can sense, think, feel, want, or do what, where, when and how. For example, many couples have rules in their relationship which say they cannot *directly* talk about important issues in their relationship. Couples who adhere to this rule leave the development of their relationship to chance and indirect communication. Figure 7-1 represents a couple limited to this type of an ongoing interaction.

Figure 7-1   Ongoing Interaction

On the other hand, there is an increasing number of couples who want to be more in charge of their lives together. They have rules in their relationship which say they can be completely and congruently aware of themselves and their partner and talk directly about their awareness. Figure 7-2 represents this kind of couple who do periodically step outside the circle of their ongoing interaction and look at how they relate.

Figure 7-2   Meta-talk

In effect, this couple can "meta-talk." They can step outside their routine interaction and look at where they've been, where they are and where they're going in relation to any issue. Frequently, meta-talk is done with the notion of altering some of their ordinary routines, to make life more satisfactory and productive for both partners.

How does this relate to the issues of agreement/disagreement discussed earlier? Well, achieving agreement about rules for dealing with issues is very important. *In order for a relationship to grow and develop, consensus must be established around rules for dealing with issues.*

When both partners agree not to talk directly about issues important to them, they have procedural consensus. It may be possible to have a satisfactory relationship with this arrangement, and it may provide stability, but little capacity for dealing with new situations creatively is provided. On the other hand, partners who mutually consent to some procedure for dealing directly with their awareness can also enjoy a mutually-satisfying relationship. However, their relationship is potentially more viable—capable of both stability and flexibility—since they have underlying predictable rules which support them in making choices about how they're going to deal with the new information and new situations which bring variety into their lives.

Both our research and experience indicate that chronically troubled partnerships are characterized by lack of agreement and consensus about procedures for dealing with issues in their relationship. Usually one partner wants to deal with an issue and the other one doesn't. Or both partners take turns wanting to and not wanting to so that when he wants to, she doesn't, and when she wants to, he doesn't. As a result, they never simultaneously decide either to deal with something or not to deal with something. This kind of relationship is very often unsatisfactory for one or both partners.

Figure 7-3 adds a basic ingredient to the topic, personal, relationship issue spectrum. While you can have disagreement and variety around issues, agreement is important when it comes to the procedural rules for dealing with issues. Without this solid foundation, the relationship is both rigid and uncertain. And frequently topical, personal and relationship issues become confused with each other.

Figure 7-3 The Relationship Between Issues
and Procedural Rules

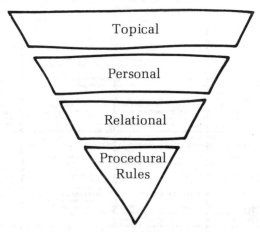

Before talking about practical aspects of dealing with issues—what we call "procedure setting"—we want to point out that, in addition to a *lack of consensus* about procedure, *confusion between issues and procedures* can create difficulty in dealing with issues.

For example, one partner confuses the other's interest in talking about an issue with the other's *willingness* to talk about an issue at a particular place or point in time:

Larry: "I wisl. ou'd quit smoking, it really bothers me."

Jill: "Don't throw that at me just as I'm relaxed ready to fall asleep. What are you trying to do? That ticks me off!"

Here Jill may be interested in dealing with the issue (Larry's dislike of her smoking), but she doesn't want to do it at that particular time and place. By the way she responded to him, he might jump to the conclusion that she never wants to talk about how her smoking bothers him. This is how easy it is to confuse issue and procedure.

PROCEDURE SETTING

In practical terms, what goes into "procedure setting?" Literally it involves paying particular attention to several factors when one or both partners have an issue they'd like to talk about and deal with directly. Procedure setting is a way of assuring readiness to focus on an issue. Figure 7-4 lists the factors to be considered when you set procedures.

Figure 7-4   Factors In Procedure Setting

Issue	what
Procedure	whose
	who
	where
	how
	energy
	length
	stopping

This is what we mean by each of these factors:

1. *What* to talk about.

   That "what" represents the issue itself. It can be a topic, personal or relationship issue of either or both partners. Establishing agreement about what it is you want to talk about is a good starting point.

2. *Whose* issue it is.

   Here it's important to identify whose issue it is primarily: mine, yours, ours, someone else's or no one's. This is particularly important when an issue is mine and does not involve you, but I want you to be a consultant to my concern.

3. *Who* is included.

   Another important consideration is who is to be included in the discussion. Sometimes the two of you want to be alone away from friends or members of your family. Other times, you'll want certain people present. For instance, "I'd like to have the children hear us talk about this." Generally, you'll find yourself reserving certain discussions to include or exclude certain people.

4. *Where* to talk.

   Place is important. There are some places conducive to

focusing on important issues but other places can be quite distracting.

5. *When* to talk.

Timing is extremely important. At certain times, you simply don't have enough time to start something and be able to follow it sufficiently to bring it to closure. Trying to force an issue into an inadequate time slot usually generates more tension and dissonance. On the other hand, when both partners want to deal with something even though time is limited, it's surprising how much can be accomplished when both focus together around the issue, as Amy and Don did earlier in this chapter.

6. *How* we talk.

How two people talk is reflected in their styles of communication. (We have devoted all of Section 3 to this.)

7. *Energy* available for dealing with the issue.

Even with all the other conditions right, sometimes physical or mental fatigue dominates. Often the solution to issues is closely related to the energy you put into exploring and focusing. Some issues are best reserved to times when you have energy to handle them. However, chronically low energy may suggest you're avoiding some issue or some dimension of your awareness.

8. *Length* of discussion.

Here it's important that partners have a sense about how much time they want to spend on an issue before they either resolve it or decide to stop for awhile, then pick up on it again at another time. Some partners seem to have issues they frequently deal with indirectly but never resolve. Part of the reason for this is they don't put themselves more in charge of how much time they're going to spend on an issue.

9. *Stopping* the discussion.

This factor is closely related to length of discussion. It's important that couples have some common rule for stopping a discussion when one or both partners wants to do so. For example, "Let's talk until the news comes on and quit." "Either one of us can say, 'hey, I'd like to stop,' okay?" Being able to punctuate dealing with your issues in terms of starting and stopping will allow you time for both dealing with issues and playing comfortably, knowing that important issues have their time and place for getting proper attention.

Looking at all these factors, you must be wondering if two people can ever simultaneously agree to all of them at one point in time! Actually, we're not suggesting that it is necessary to run down this list each time you want to deal with an issue. But occasionally it is important to structure an issue by taking these factors into account. More often though, it's enough to be aware that a discussion may not be productive if one of these factors is out of alignment. For example, you might want to talk about a particular issue with your partner alone except you really don't have the energy to take it on at that point. In this case, being able to say this to your partner can clarify your temporary disinterest in the issue.

Most important, however, is that when a discussion is not progressing, it's often useful to think in terms of procedure. Frequently discussions fail because procedures are out of line. Someone is trying to do something he doesn't want to do at that time or place, and it's reflected in the interaction.

So tune into procedures. They're important. And before beginning a serious discussion, set up the ground rules. Share a meaning with your partner around what it is you want. Check out your procedures with your partner before getting into sharing your awareness about the issue. The procedures you and your partner adopt go a long way toward supporting the growth of your relationship. If you consistently try to violate procedures when dealing with issues, e.g., by bringing up issues at inappropriate times, in improper places, with people not involved in your relationship, you may destroy your relationship itself. Most systems have procedures for maintaining their boundaries, discussing some issues only in private, etc. Maintaining boundaries plays an important part in making a relationship intimate and unique.

In summary, agreement is important in a relationship, particularly around rules of the relationship. Many partners confuse issues with the procedures they use for dealing with the issues, and tensions result. Some partners never develop their relationship to its optimum because they can't agree on procedures for looking at everyday issues. Others, unwittingly, fail to agree on procedures in order to avoid looking at real conflicts in their partnership. But when you and your partner can form a consensus on your procedures for handling issues, you've often done half the job. That's because the spirit of willingness to focus and support each other is a powerful force in a relationship itself. And when it's present, relationships can use disagreements and differences for growing.

KEY IDEAS FROM SECTION TWO

1. Maintaining awareness of others is just as important as maintaining self-awareness for effective interpersonal communication.

2. Using the skill of checking out can increase your awareness of others.

3. The shared meaning process helps both sender and receiver increase the accuracy of communication. It involves self-disclosure skills and several others:

   Stating intention and asking for acknowledgement

   Acknowledging the sender's message

   Confirming/clarifying

4. Messages can focus on a topic, self, partner or relationship.

5. Issues in partnerships can be topical, personal, or relationship.

6. Both understanding and agreement are important in relationships; agreement is particularly important around rules for talking about issues.

7. Procedure setting is important for establishing the context discussing an issue.

STYLES OF COMMUNICATION

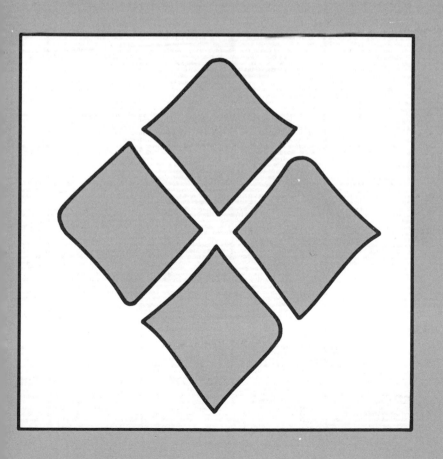

In the following section, we will describe four different styles of verbal communication; four different ways of talking. Each of these styles will be described in terms of the intentions people typically have when they use the style and the behaviors they use to express the style. The styles discussion in the first two chapters of this section will focus on what the styles look like when they are "pure." But actually, much of the time people communicate with mixed styles, so the last chapter will describe those kinds of messages.

In these chapters, we will also comment on when a particular style is useful and when it isn't. Our discussion may appear to suggest that one style—Style IV—is the "good" one, and all the rest are the "bad" ones, because of our belief that Style IV is especially important when you and your partner want to clarify and deal with a significant personal or relationship issue. In this kind of situation, Style IV is unmatched for enabling you and your partner to share your Awareness Wheels and focus directly on an issue.

Nevertheless, after reading these chapters, we hope you will have an appreciation for the appropriate and inappropriate uses of each style. We have mentioned several times that a limited communicator is usually a less effective communicator. This principle also applies to styles. A person with only a limited repertoire of communication styles has a difficult time expressing his awareness effectively.

CHAPTER EIGHT

THREE STYLES OF COMMUNICATION

We've noticed a curious and interesting happening between partners. Most partners think that they can change the nature of their discussion simply by shifting their focus, by changing what they talk about. While changing what you talk about has an impact, your messages are most dramatically changed by shifting style; by shifting *how* you talk about something.[1] And how you talk about something depends to a large extent on what your intentions are. So, we're going to talk about three styles, how they connect with your intentions, and what behaviors go along with each style. A word of caution: for each style we're going to present a list of behaviors. Don't try to memorize the list, but use it as a guide to help you recognize the style that you are using.

STYLE I

This friendly, sociable, playful style keeps the world going. When you want to play, or want to keep things moving in an easy and light way, you are most likely to talk in Style I.

Style I communication is essential to carrying on most ordinary, everyday activities. In this style, information is exchanged in a way that meets social expectations. Usually, the speaker's intentions are to be pleasant and polite and not to change anything. There is a wish to communicate in a comfortable way. Several dimensions of

[1]Material presented in this section is a modification and elaboration of William F. Hill, *Hill Interaction Matrix: Scoring Manual* (Los Angeles: Univ. of So. Calif., Youth Studies Center, 1961).

the Awareness Wheel may be involved in Style I messages. For example, sensations may be described, or thoughts, or preferences shared. And action statements often occur in the telling of anecdotes or reporting of events. But direct disclosure of immediate and intimate feelings and intentions are almost always missing.

Many Style I statements suggest positive pairing between the two people involved. They indirectly demonstrate the basic fondness and attraction the two feel for one another. For example, two people joking are showing "evidence" of their mutual affection without saying directly, "I like you, I have fun with you," etc.

Figure 8-1. Intentions in Style I.

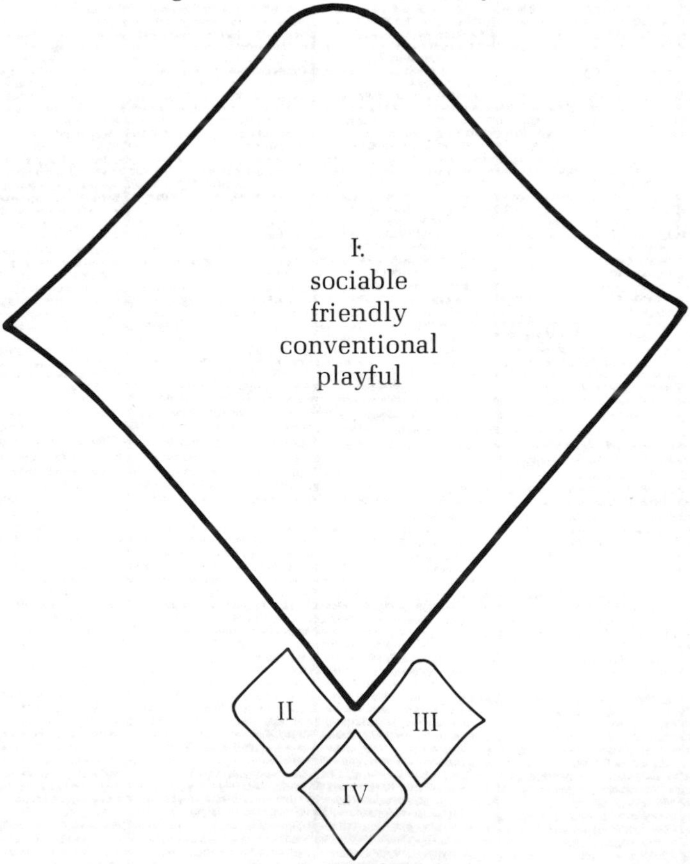

I.
sociable
friendly
conventional
playful

II   III

IV

Behaviors.

Chit chat/small talk; passing time:

"How's your golf game these days?"

"Boy, time flies. The new car models are out already."

Amenities:

"How are you today?"

"It's been a long time since I've seen you."

Simple descriptions:

"I notice you're wearing a new sweater."

"You dropped your pencil."

Reporting of events:

"George came over today and left a couple of records."

"We went to the game last night. The Gophers won again."

Factual information:

"The store closes at 5 p.m. today."

"Twelve people have signed up to go."

Story-telling; Anecdotes:

"You wouldn't believe what happened to me today. I was walking . . ."

"Did you hear the one about . . ."

Non-hostile joking:

"The nice thing about my car is it's small enough to push when it conks out."

"Who do you think you are—Howard Cosell?"

Unelaborated statements about:

—Simple preferences:

"I'd like to go to the farm this weekend."

"I'd prefer the green shirt over the blue one."

—Opinions:

"I think the Mets are a better team than they've shown so far."

"I suspect the government will be deficit spending for many years to come."

—Values:

"I'd travel anywhere in the country at the drop of a hat."

"My friends are really important to me."

—Attitudes:

"I'm a firm believer in equal pay for equal work."

"I don't really care if we don't go."

—Possessions:

"That's a beautiful jacket."

"Do you want to borrow my car?"

—Physical/feeling states:

"I'm tired and hungry."

"This room seems cold to me."

References to:

—Relatively fixed appearances:

"What do you weigh now?"

"Your hair must really be healthy, it sure seems to grow fast."

—Biographical data:

> "I grew up in Denver."

> "I've got two sisters and a brother."

—Personal traits:

> "You seem to have a lot of energy."

> "I enjoy your sense of humor."

—Habits, routines:

> "I seldom miss breakfast."

> "I don't seem to be able to quit smoking."

—Activities:

> "I'll go buy the groceries on my way home."

> "When we finish doing the dishes, let's go to the movie."

Characteristic Language.

Personal Pronouns—I, me, my, mine:

> *—with description of observations or actions:*

>> *"I just saw John a couple minutes ago."*

>> *"I can't remember seeing a more stunning sunset."*

> *—with, sociable, "everyday" expressions of intentions and feelings:*

>> *"I like to play tennis rather than golf."*

>> *"I'd like to go shopping before supper."*

>> *"I'm feeling relaxed now. There's nothing like a hot shower."*

>> *"I can call you later."*

Vocal Characteristics.

normal

relaxed tone

tension-free

friendly

Typical Style I Conversation.

Paul: "Good seeing you again. I haven't seen you for—when was the last time?"

Jill: "Probably at the party that night."

Paul: "What party was that? Oh, at my place. That's right."

Jill: "I stopped over last weekend when you were gone."

Paul: "Sorry I missed you."

Jill: "I really like your shoes. Where'd you get those?"

Paul: "Like those, huh? At a store up north. Just saw them in the window and liked them."

Jill: "Special kind of store? I've never seen any like that."

Paul: "I don't think so, you know, they've got just a lot of ordinary shoes and then I saw these."

Jill: "And those."

Paul: "Uh, I like the kind of mocassin effect."

Jill: "Yeah, I've never seen any like that."

Paul: "They're really comfortable, uh, soft inside, kind of like a slipper. I thought they'd wear out real easy, but they haven't."

Jill: "I think you've got good taste."

Paul: "Thanks. What have you been doing lately?"

Jill: "Getting tired of working. I don't like working in the summer. I really don't like it. So I'm going to take a vacation."

Paul: "Are you going to travel somewhere?"

Jill: "Out to Oregon. I'm going to borrow a tent and some camping equipment and just go out slowly. Before when I went to California, I got there in two days."

Paul: "You just drove straight through?"

Jill: "Practically. I stayed in a motel at night. But that really is no way to go."

Paul: "I think I'm going to take a vacation, too—not sure where though."

Jill: "Uh-huh."

Paul: "I'm enjoying my work right now though. I've got a lot of energy going for it. Enjoying what I'm doing."

Jill: "Yeah, sounds like you're excited about it."

Paul: "Well I'm finishing some things up now but by the end of summer I'll be ready for a holiday."

Jill: "Uh-huh."

You probably recognize in your own communication the kinds of statements illustrated here. After all, there are hundreds of things we talk about while we keep our lives moving along smoothly, or just enjoy being together. You may have noticed also that most of the skills we talked about in the first two sections of the book are missing. That's because most of these aren't necessary with Style I. Other than "speaking for self," you really don't have to bother much about skills when you're using this style. Style I can be used to express any focus, but usually the focus is topical.

Style I is a good one for maintaining topic focus, or for having fun. But when an issue exists—when something is bothering you and you want to talk about it, or when something about your relationship with your partner is a concern, Style I is not helpful. Style I statements disclose little about yourself. If you and your partner attempt to discuss important issues in Style I, you'll probably sound detached and disconnected from what's happening.

In the following sample, notice how irrelevant Marge and John's discussion seems to be, when you keep in mind that there's a relationship issue Marge wants to deal with. Marge usually ends up being responsible for making plans for the time she and John spend together. She becomes quite annoyed with John about this. They had planned to go to a movie and Marge wanted John to speak up more clearly about his preferences:

> Marge: "There are several good movies in town this week. Which one would you prefer?"
>
> John: "Any of them would be fine."
>
> Marge: "Wouldn't you like to pick one tonight?"
>
> John: "You can choose. It's okay with me."
>
> Marge: "Okay."

In this example, Style I just isn't doing the job. Marge's intention is to let John know she wants him to make a decision and that she's annoyed with his indecisiveness. Without disclosing her feelings, intentions, and interpretation of their pattern directly to John, she won't be able to clarify the issue. To do these things requires a different style.

STYLE II

Even though II is right next to I numerically, there's a world of difference between them. The intentions connected with Style II do not simply involve keeping things moving smoothly. Rather, Style II usually has the intention of forcing change in another person or in a situation—shooting for a certain outcome. Most Style II statements involve interpretations (who or what's right/wrong) and actions (what you should/should not do). Style II is usually used when you want to be persuasive or want to try to control what is happening or what will happen.

In everyday conversations, Style II is very common and it's not all unfriendly. When you want to compliment, praise, persuade, or direct, this is a natural style to use. In fact, it would be impossible to exist without Style II! (That's a Style II statement in itself.) Most selling, bargaining, promoting, advocating, preaching, and lecturing revolve around Style II communication.

In many ways, Style II is useful and appropriate. But in trying to deal with relationship issues, it can be disastrous! But before we talk more about its uses, let's look at Style II more closely.

Figure 8-2. Intentions in Style II.

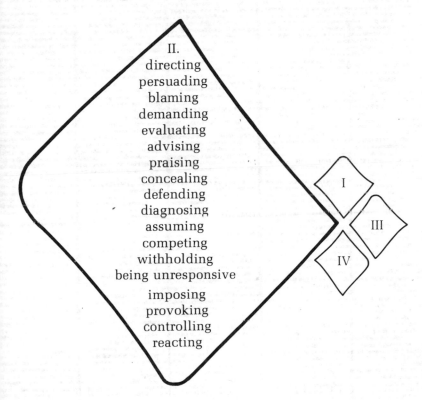

II.
directing
persuading
blaming
demanding
evaluating
advising
praising
concealing
defending
diagnosing
assuming
competing
withholding
being unresponsive
imposing
provoking
controlling
reacting

I

III

IV

Behaviors.

Directing; ordering; demanding:

"Don't talk to me like that!"

"Stop it right now!"

"We've got to increase sales by at least 10%!"

Labeling:

"You're stupid."

"He's a perfect child."

Praising:
> "Nice work; you've done a fine job."
> "That painting of yours is excellent."

Persuading; advocating:
> "Come on, let's try it just once."
> "It's really a great idea if you'll just listen."

Unchecked assumptions:
> "You never really intended to talk to him about it!"
> "You've always wanted to do it my way before."

Evaluating; judging; stereotyping (put downs):
> "You're wrong again!"
> "You're always smarter than I am."
> "That's a stupid thing to say!"
> "Only a woman would do that."

Blaming; accusing; criticizing; fault-finding:
> "You always take so much time getting dressed that you make us late."
> "You didn't care how I felt or you would have considered me."

Ventilation:
> "Damn it, don't you know it always happens this way?"
> "Who's he to tell me what to do!"

Needling; demeaning:
> "You know so much—how would you do it?"
> "Tell me how you're feeling right now. Go ahead, just tell me!"
> "But you're so young and inexperienced."

Pronouncing:

> "Men will never understand women."

> "Staying in school is the smartest thing you can do."

Pseudo questions (closed, indirect questions aimed at forcing agreement):

> "Don't you think that . . . ?"

> "Why don't you want to . . . ?"

> "Would you agree that . . . ?"

> "Will you tell me what's so terrible about how I dress?"[1]

Prescribing solutions:

> "Here's what you do . . . "

> "It will all work out if you just do as I say."

Complaining; defeatism:

> "I do all the dirty work around here and never get any help."

> "I wish things would go my way just once."

Self-protecting; disqualifying; tricking; defending:

> "That's not what I said!"

> "I didn't mean that!"

> "If you can think of a better way, tell me."

Pseudo-intellectualizing; psychologyizing; diagnosing:

> "I suggest you find the real cause of your defensiveness."

> "It would help you if you understood the problem better before trying to solve it."

> "You're paranoid."

---

[1]For an excellent discussion and exercise in misuses of questions see J. William Pfeiffer and John E. Jones, "Don't you think that . . .?" An Experimental Lecture on Indirect and Direct Communication in *The 1974 Annual Handbook for Group Facilitators*, ed., Pfeiffer & Jones (La Jolla, California: University Associates Publishers, Inc., 1974), p. 203-19.

Ignoring by changing topics; interrupting; or not listening:
    Man: "Is something bothering you?"
    Woman: (silence) "Let's eat out tonight."
    Man: "I really want to know, is . . . (interrupted by woman)
    Woman: "Where should we go?"

Indirect avoiding; non-commital; withholding:
    "I don't know; perhaps I will."
    "Well . . . maybe, I'll think about it."
    "I'll get to it when I have time."

"Acting-out" feelings:
    Grabs partner, hugs and kisses.
    Swears.
    Turns back on partner and refuses to talk.

Characteristic Language.
Speaking for others:
    "You don't know what you want from me."
    "We always have a good time together."
    "You know you like it when I'm firm with you."

Speaking for no one:
    "That's important."
    "Anyone can do that."

Key words – "should, ought, have to, need to:"
    "You really ought to be more honest with me."
    "I need your love."

Superlatives; "always, never, every, etc.:"
    "You're always there when I need you."

"Every time we're out somewhere you lose something."

"You never listen to me!"

"Right-wrong; good-bad:"

"That's the wrong way to do it."

"That's the best thing you ever said to me."

Closed, indirect questions:

"Don't you think you'd feel better if you did it my way?"

"You like being with me, don't you?"

"Won't it be a lot more fun if they come along?"

"Why" questions that demand, blame, challenge:

"Why shouldn't you do that?"

"Why do you make me so upset?"

"Why do you always say that?"

Imperatives:

"Have dinner ready when I get home."

"Stop crying."

"Don't do that to me."

"Watch out for that car!"

Vocal Characteristics.

firm

authoritative

harsh

threatening or sarcastic tone

loud

closed and negative sounding or soft, whiny, seductive

rapid rate

emotionally-charged

Style II conversation.

Here are Paul and Jill again, only this time their conversation has shifted to Style II and has become more personal and relationship-focused.

> *Paul:* "How come you kind of play games with me a lot?"
>
> *Jill:* "I don't know what you're talking about."
>
> *Paul:* "Yes, you do."
>
> *Jill:* "No, I don't."
>
> *Paul:* "That's kind of a game right there—saying you don't know what I'm talking about, when you do."
>
> *Jill:* "Well, how am I supposed to know what you're talking about if you won't tell me?"
>
> *Paul:* "We've talked about this before."
>
> *Jill:* "Not to my recollection."
>
> *Paul:* "You're kidding me!"
>
> *Jill:* "Could you explain yourself any more than what you're doing?"
>
> *Paul:* "Well—If you don't know what I'm talking about, I'm not going to tell you. I mean, how come you're avoiding what I'm talking about?"
>
> *Jill:* "You're not very clear—just making a lot of assumptions."
>
> *Paul:* "Well—"
>
> *Jill:* "I don't see how you even have the right to say anything like that—that really ticks me off."
>
> *Paul:* "So you do know what I'm talking about."
>
> *Jill:* "I think you're the one that plays games."
>
> *Paul:* "How do I play games?"
>
> *Jill:* "Um. Not being straight at all—with people."
>
> *Paul:* "I think I've been pretty straight with you."
>
> *Jill:* "You have not! I can't imagine how you have any decent relationships with anybody."

Paul: "That's off the subject. I'm just talking about the way we get along. Not trying to—generalize or something."

Jill: "Well, I could imagine—that if you respond the same way to everybody that you do to me."

Paul: "Well, what I'm thinking about is that time when I poked you in the back and you got all upset. I was just trying to—have some fun."

How many different kinds of Style II behaviors can you identify in Paul and Jill's conversation? We think their conversation will sound familiar, somehow, to most of you—because most of us have had lots of exposure to Style II communication—both hearing it and using it.

The Style II intentions we listed have a rather negative aspect. We don't usually think of ourselves as trying to "force change in another person; "prescribe solutions," avoid taking responsibility for our own awareness." But often we do. And when we do, it's probably because we think it will be effective in achieving our goals, or because we don't have a more appropriate style in our repertory.

When you try to use Style II to deal with a relationship issue, it seldom helps you to achieve your purposes. Keep in mind that the intention in Style II is usually to force change or control the outcome and this can kill creativity and vitality in the relationship. Most people resist pressures to change because the underlying message often is "You're wrong," or "Me first," or "I value my goals more than I value you," or "I don't need to change, you do!" With resistance, comes the temptation to increase the pressure. If you begin to apply more pressure to force change, Style II can easily backfire and explode into conflict. The result is often increased misunderstanding and hurt feelings between the two of you—and a temporary distancing.

However, Style II explosions and fights do not have to be disastrous for relationships. In fact, Style II messages about relationship issues can be useful in signaling that there are areas of significant tension. And when Style II messages occur in the middle of an ongoing discussion of a relationship issue, they can serve the function of letting off a little emotional steam. But if the boiler really bursts, and you begin attacking your partner's sense of self-worth, you can usually forget about dealing with the issue constructively at that point.

In short, the real danger is not simply in using Style II—that's normal. Rather, the biggest danger—and it is a significant and real one—is that after partners try to deal with issues in Style II and find that they can't, they give up trying and fail to deal with issues at all. Sometimes this occurs because of their fear of fighting and hurting each other, but more often, perhaps, because partners have only limited communication skills and cannot move beyond Style II. Whatever the reason, trying to bury significant personal and relationship issues by ignoring them can lead to even greater difficulty, because the issues have a way of not staying buried. In fact, they tend to pop up in all sorts of unexpected ways, providing a constant source of tension in the relationship.

Some partnerships are stuck in the dilemma of having only the two alternatives: (1) ignoring issues and living with the tension, or (2) trying to deal with them using Style II, which usually results in quarrels, misunderstandings, and hurt feelings. But this doesn't have to be the case. Other communication styles are available for effectively dealing with issues. We'll talk about them in the remainder of this chapter and in the next one. But before that, we want to say a few more words about Style II.

We have seen that Style II has destructive potential when partners attempt to use it in dealing with different issues. Recognize, however, that *all* of us use Style II at one time or another. We use it, for example, when our intention is to change something (usually another person) or to try to control a situation; when we want to prescribe solutions to issues; when our emotions are at a high level and awareness is low; when, for any number of reasons, we simply don't want to try to deal with an issue. So, using Style II does happen; it's natural, and we needn't be too surprised when we find ourselves using it.

When you choose to use Style II, however, recognize that it is a *limiting* style. It limits the possibility of effectively dealing with an issue; in fact, it may change the focus away from the issue. So if your intention is to help you and your partner clarify an issue, disclose self and be receptive to each others' self-disclosures, Style

II isn't likely to help you. Rather, it is likely to work against your intentions.

STYLE III

As we have seen when your world is fairly smooth and running the way you want it to, you tend to communicate in Style I. When you begin to think you'd like some change to occur or you think something is changing without your consent, or when your expectations begin to change or become unclear, you're likely to shift to Style II.

The intentions involved in Style III are quite different from those of Styles I and II. Rather than trying to keep things smooth, or to change and control, the intention in Style III is almost to stop your world, reflect on it, and explore it, to look at an issue or event and see what's behind it, what has happened in the past or can happen in the future. It's a tentative and speculative style.

Figure 8-3. Intentions in Style III.

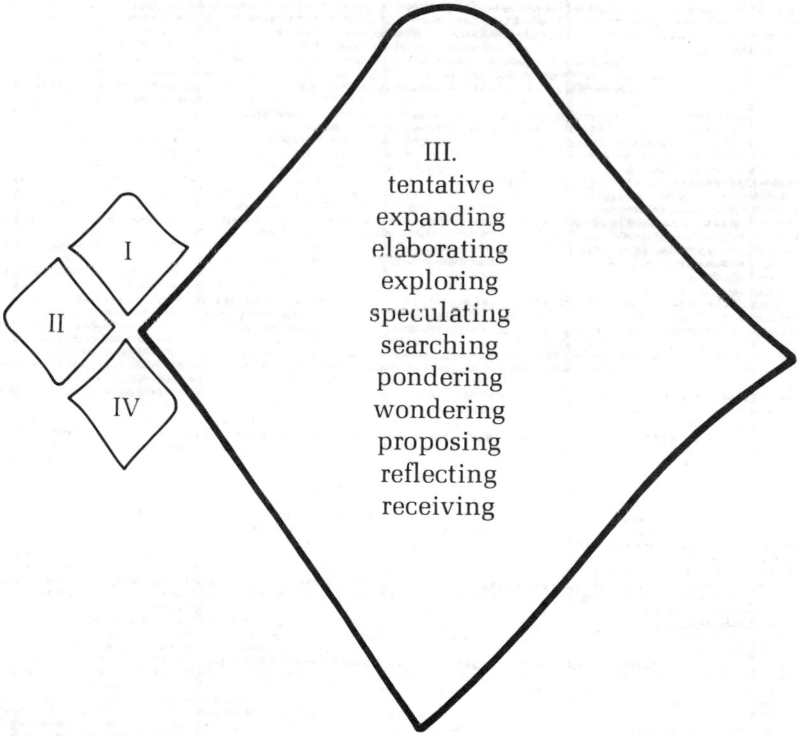

III.
tentative
expanding
elaborating
exploring
speculating
searching
pondering
wondering
proposing
reflecting
receiving

I

II

IV

Behaviors.

Giving Impressions about:

—personal qualities:

"Sometimes I get the impression you're preoccupied with other things."

"I believe you are a thoughtful person."

"I wonder why you're so quiet tonight."

—interpersonal dynamics:

"Could there be some competition between us?"

"Sometimes I think you're over-protecting me."

"It seems to me we've been this way for a long time."

Giving explanations:

"I usually do that when I'm uncertain. Do you know what I mean?"

"My moods seem to fluctuate. Maybe that's why I'm difficult to figure out sometimes."

Speculating about causes:

"Do you think you're tired today because of our fight last night?"

"Maybe our relationship works so well because we have many of the same interests."

Searching for reasons:

"I wonder if it's because I've been working nights recently."

"I think it might have to do with the way you grew up."

Posing analyses:

"I think our arguments about money may be related to a bigger issue."

"Many men seem to have the same attitude."

Posing solutions and alternatives:

"Maybe we could develop a budget to control our spending better."

"What would you think about talking to the kids about this?"

Offering kindly advice:

"Have you tried doing anything about it?" (Caution—advice is seldom given in a straight Style III message. It is usually given in Style II or as a mixed message [Style II mixed with Style III.].

Inviting and encouraging others to supply information with open questions:

"Would you tell me what you're thinking?"

"How do you see it?"

"Would you explain what you mean by that?"

"What gives you that impression?"

Supportive reflection:

"I guess you must be feeling pretty bored doing that all day."

"It seems to me you've really been working hard lately."

(Caution—in attempting to be supportive, it is easy to slip into speaking for the other and making closed assumptions about them.)

"There and then," past or future time orientation:

"What would happen if we tried that sometime?"

"It seems like we used to have some good times together."

Procedural comments:

"I have something I'd like to talk to you about."

"Could we set some time aside tonight?"

"What is it you want to talk about?"

Characteristic Language.

"Checking out" with direct open questions (who, what, where, when, how type questions which are non-challenging):

"What do you think?"

"How do you want to do it?"

Qualifiers such as probably, maybe, sometimes, perhaps, hopefully, could, might:

"We probably don't listen to each other."

"Maybe we would enjoy taking separate vacations."

Qualified self-disclosures:

"I think I like it when you do that."

"I was probably mad at you just then."

Vocal Characteristics.

calm
quiet tone
a bit hesitant

Style III conversation.

Here Paul and Jill continue to talk about their relationship, only this time in Style III.

Paul: "I kind of think we like each other a lot, you know, enjoy getting together, but I don't know. What happens sometimes— it seems like we misunderstand each other. Things get mixed up. Do you know what goes on?"

Jill: "I can't really understand why we might have a hard time understanding each other sometimes. Maybe when we first see each other we aren't used to each other for a bit."

Paul: "I'm not sure what you mean."

Jill: "It probably just takes a while getting comfortable with each other again."

Paul: "Yeah, that might be."

Jill: "Have you got any new ideas about it?"

Paul: "Yeah, I was just thinking, sometimes, well, sometimes I guess I'm not sure how you feel about me, whether you like me or enjoy seeing me and so that kind of gets in the way."

Jill: "Uh huh. Go on."

Paul: "Oh, and I think one thing might be that we've had different relationships over time. We've known each other, you know first as for awhile a student relationship and then we worked together and now we don't see each other so regularly because we're not working together. It's more friendship and I guess maybe I'm not, you know, really sure."

Jill: "What, exactly the relationship is?"

Paul: "Yeah, maybe."

Like Styles I and II, Style III makes only limited use of the skills described in the first part of the book. Style III uses the skill of speaking for self, with lots of statements beginning with "I," but most of them are "I think." In this style, the interpretation dimension of the Awareness Wheel is used heavily. Action statements also are used quite a bit, but these tend to be descriptions of past behaviors, or tentative proposals for future actions (such as, "I have . . . , Maybe I will . . . "). Style III includes practically no feeling or intention statements, and little documentation. On the other hand, Style III makes liberal use of checking out, (for example, "What do you think about. . . ? Would it be useful to . . . ?").

Style III, along with Style II, may focus on either self, partner, or relationship issues. But when a Style III exchange does focus on a personal or relationship issue, it's usually handled in a safe way, with a tendency to discuss past events or possible future events. There is little disclosure of "what's happening right now" and no commitment to take *action*; to do something about the issue. In short, Style III typically expresses a commitment to deal with an issue cognitively, at the interpretive level, but there is little emotion or commitment to take action based on current awareness.

Nevertheless, Style III is a useful one, extremely helpful in achieving several purposes in the process of dealing with issues. First, it can help identify and clarify issues you and your partner want to talk about.

> *Larry:* "I don't think we've been having much fun together lately. What do you think?"
>
> *Joanne:* "Now that you mention it, I think that's probably right. Especially when we're with other people."
>
> *Larry:* "Maybe that's something worth exploring a bit."

Second, Style III is useful for examining background information relevant to the issue.

> *Joanne:* (continuing the conversation): "Could it have anything to do with the fact that most of your friends have moved away? So we've been spending most of our time lately with my friends?"
>
> *Larry:* "It might. When I was younger, I always had a hard time making friends."

And third, Style III might be useful in generating alternative courses of action.

> *Joanne:* "Well, if that's true, maybe I could pay more attention to you when we're with other people. Do you think it would help if I did more of that?"
>
> *Larry:* "Maybe it would. And how would it be if we looked for some friends who weren't yours or mine, but were ours."
>
> *Joanne:* "We could try that, too."

To summarize briefly, Style III is useful in the process of dealing with issues. It can be helpful in raising issues; in this respect, it is similar to Style II. But unlike Style II, which tends to result in premature demands for solution, shifts in focus away from the issue, and leads to conflict, Style III can contribute toward effective resolution of issues by exploring relevant background information and proposing possible actions. However, because feelings, intentions, and future actions are expressed only tentatively—or not at all Style III by itself is also a limited style. Style III doesn't move to the core of issues. Style IV adds this essential dimension.

OVERVIEW OF STYLE DIFFERENCES

The three styles differ in two ways: intentions and behaviors. The intentions accompanying Style I are the everyday intentions to keep your world running smoothly. To do that, you keep most of the information in your Awareness Wheel to yourself, and you eliminate personal or relationship issues from your focus, concentrating instead on non-issue subjects. When your intentions are to change somebody, you're most likely to use Style II. Issues surface, but are not identified, clarified, and dealt with completely and congruently. In Style II you are usually trying to force change or control outcomes. When your intention is to understand, you most often use Style III. This style identifies an issue at an intellectual level and expands on it, involving the sifting of ideas and causes, and exploring past and future possibilities.

As with intentions, the behaviors used in these styles differ quite a lot, too. Both Styles I and II are low in self-disclosure. Style I makes fairly heavy use of sensory data: "I saw a robin today. First one I've seen this spring." There is chit chatting and describing events and things seen. Style II makes few sense statements, and uses only a small part of the Awareness Wheel, most often interpretations. When feelings and intentions are expressed in Style II, they are more likely "acted out," indirectly, leaving the receiver to guess at what is meant. While Style III involves clearer identification of an issue, self-disclosure is not complete. It focuses most heavily on interpretations with some disclosures of sensation and actions. Style III disclosures of feelings and intentions are stated tentatively, or else focus on the past rather than immediate feelings and intentions. However, Style III does disclose more self-information directly about an issue than Style I or Style II.

Styles II and III can also be viewed as *transitional* styles. When an issue arises, unless it's identified directly and a procedure is set to deal with it, partners usually move into Style II as a way of indirectly *signaling*, "I've got an issue," or into Style III as a way of safely "testing the water" before really getting into the issue. If there is a great deal of Style II or III talk in your partnership, you or your partner may have some issues which neither of you are dealing with directly. Here is where Style IV is useful—the style most likely to disclose completely your own awareness and focus on your contribution to the relationship. We move to this style in the next chapter.

Before we leave this chapter, take a couple of minutes, if you haven't already done so, and think about how you and your partner use these three styles. Which do you use most frequently? In what situations? What, if anything, do you think this says about your relationship and your effectiveness as communicators?

CHAPTER NINE

STYLE IV: A COMMITTED STYLE

When an issue exists for you or partner, you may have a number of different intentions regarding it. One may be to avoid dealing with the issue so as not to rock the boat. You will most likely carry out this intention by communicating in Style I. Another intention you may have is to create change in your partner. If so, you will most likely express it with Style II behavior. A third intention might be to explore the issue and develop a general understanding of it, often by disclosing some background information or by speculating about future possibilities. This kind of intention is typically expressed in Style III.

Another distinct alternative for dealing with an issue is Style IV Communication, which expresses a different set of intentions from those in any of the previously-mentioned styles. In Style IV, intentions and behaviors demonstrate a *commitment* to deal *completely* and *congruently* with an issue. Let's continue to follow Paul and Jill as they talk to each other about their relationship in Style IV.

> *Paul:* "Jill, I like you a lot. Part of it's because I think you're really straight with me. Like the last time I saw you and was teasing you, and you didn't think it was so funny and told me so. I was surprised at your reaction and a bit embarrassed, but I liked it that you let me know this."

Jill: "Yeah, I was amazed that I reacted that way. You know, I didn't really have time to think about it. That week I had been hassled at work by some men teasing me and doing some things I thought were kind of demeaning. When you teased me, I exploded kind of unjustly at you. But I felt comfortable doing that because I didn't think I always have to be pleasant and things do come out from where I'm at that aren't always so nice."

Paul: "Okay, that's the part about being straight I like. You don't just laugh it off."

Jill: "I also felt pretty confident about just doing that with you because I knew that it wouldn't change any part of our relating."

Paul: "Yeah, well, in that situation I was trying to say I like you, but wasn't being very straight about it. I want to be more straight with you but find myself doing other things. In the future, I'm going to try to be more direct with you."

Jill: "I'd like that."

This may be unfamiliar, maybe even a strange style of communication for you. For most people, it's a more direct way of talking to someone than they learned when growing up. Many people use all of the behaviors from Style IV at one time or another, but they seldom pull them all together in the same conversation to share a complete picture of their awareness with their partner. Putting several specific behaviors together is part of what distinguishes this style from the three we have talked about so far. Style IV is also distinguished by the *intentions* associated with it. Let's look at these.

STYLE IV INTENTIONS

What do we mean about the fact that Style IV communication is characterized by a commitment to deal completely and congruently with an issue?

First, Style IV expresses an intention to *pursue the process of dealing with an issue openly and directly rather than avoiding it. Often the first step is simply setting the procedure for dealing with the issue. Saying to your partner, "I want to, or I don't want to, work on this issue at this time."*

A second essential in Style IV is being in *contact with your awareness.* Whenever you are communicating in Style IV, whether setting procedure or actually dealing with an issue, the primary focus is on yourself: what's in your awareness at that moment. This means staying in touch with your senses, your thoughts, your feelings (positive and negative), your intentions (short- and long-term for self, partner and relationship), and your actions (current as well as what you are willing to do in the future). Your attention centers on *your contribution* to the issue without being defensive and on *your own response* to your partner without blaming him/her. Being responsible for yourself is essential to Style IV communication. Any statements that begin to sound like "you're making me . . ." or "you cause me to . . . " shift the responsibility from you to your partner and you are no longer in Style IV. You are slipping into Style II communication.

As you "tune into" your self-awareness, committing yourself to the current process, a third intention is present if you allow yourself to be completely self-aware. That is, you *accept and trust* your self-awareness, even when it is difficult to do so. Sometimes you may think your awareness is so unusual or so unacceptable that you will not let yourself be completely aware. Complete awareness, particularly awareness of incongruent parts, is essential information. This awareness puts you directly in touch with your "growing edge"—the point of excitement, uncertainty or tension through which you must move if you are going to deal directly with the issue. As you accept your awareness, you are centering your energy to move effectively on the issue.

Style IV communication involves translating your awareness into words and sharing your awareness with your partner. The major intention present in Style IV communication is *to disclose* your self-awareness, fully and honestly to your partner. Sidney Jourard, who coined the term "self-disclosure," summarized the importance of disclosing yourself: "Man's behavior is visible. His inner *self* is not. Through direct and uncontrived disclosure we can begin to unveil the mystery that one man is for another. Yet, we conceal our inner *selves* to be safe from criticism, ridicule, or rejection. When a man does not acknowledge to himself and to others who he is, when he hides his inner *self* behind a wall of pretense, he is estranged equally from himself and society."[1]

Implicit in Style IV, is the intention to reveal rather than conceal yourself from your partner. Style IV discloses all parts of your Awareness Wheel.

Trying to understand your partner's self-awareness is another intention in Style IV. When you want to be, you can be intimately in contact with your partner by hearing and accepting your partner's disclosure even though you may think and feel differently from him/her about the issue. Getting in contact with your partner's awareness involves understanding him/her accurately. It does not necessarily mean agreeing with him/her, as we pointed out in Chapter 7. An accurate understanding of your partner's awareness is an essential basis for working through an issue—as important as recognizing, accepting, and disclosing your own awareness.

Another essential part of Style IV communication is your intention to *value both yourself and your partner* as you deal with an issue. In some ways this is the most important intention of Style IV, because it captures the spirit of caring and mutual support. Personal and relationship growth cannot occur if the valuing of one partner and the building of his/her esteem occurs at the expense of the other. Putting yourself down or putting your partner down undermines relationship development.

Finally, in Style IV communication you have the intention of *taking charge of your own life*, not leaving it to chance. This means, you translate your complete awareness into congruent action— acting *on* your awareness rather than acting *out* your awareness. This means aligning your senses, thoughts, feelings, and intentions with your actions, rather than seeking, thinking, feeling, and wanting one thing, and doing something completely different— divorced from your awareness. So, for example, when you feel sad, angry, or elated you make use of this self-information as a basis for making choices and acting. And as you focus on your own actions, and take responsibility for them, you do not push your partner to act, trying to force him/her to do for you what you are unwilling to do for yourself.

[1]Sidney M. Jourard, Quotation taken from the book jacket of *Self-Disclosure: An Experimental Analysis of the Transparent Self* (New York: John Wiley and Sons, Inc., 1971).

What Intentions are Missing from Style IV?

Some intentions which take you away from Style IV communication are:

—blame

—self-defense

—demanding agreement or change

—concealing awareness

Each of these intentions is closely tied in with the "win-lose" competitive spirit of *Style II* communication. If you carry these intentions with you, fail to recognize or accept them as a part of your experience, and do not disclose them directly and honestly to your partner, you will not be communicating in Style IV. Your attempts to communicate openly end up as "mixed messages." (We will have more to say about mixed messages in the next chapter.)

In essence, the intentions in Style IV are something of a paradox. As soon as you try to use Style IV behaviors to win, you lose. It doesn't work. It becomes mechanical. Win-lose intentions are simply contrary to the cooperative intentions in Style IV communication. As soon as you try to use Style IV to force change, you move out of it. One of the interesting things about Style IV, however, is that when you want your partner to change or you have some feelings of blame, and share this directly with your him/her, everything is out in the open. Then, strangely enough, you remain in Style IV.

Be careful, though, with your expectations. Just asking for something you want does not mean your partner must do it. What happens when you share these typically hidden intentions is that you create understanding with your partner and enhance trust that both of you can be honest with each other. But if your expectation is "now that I've said it, it's got to happen," you're out of Style IV into II. You cannot say to yourself, "I'm going to be in Style IV to change my partner." You *can* say, "I'm going to be in Style IV, change myself and our interaction."

In short, when I have any non-Style IV intentions which I do not express directly and honestly, I automatically slip out of Style IV.

As you can see, Style IV means candidly contacting, accepting, and disclosing yourself—who you really are at a given point in time.

A summary of the various Style IV intentions is shown in Figure 9-1:

Figure 9-1. Intentions in Style IV.

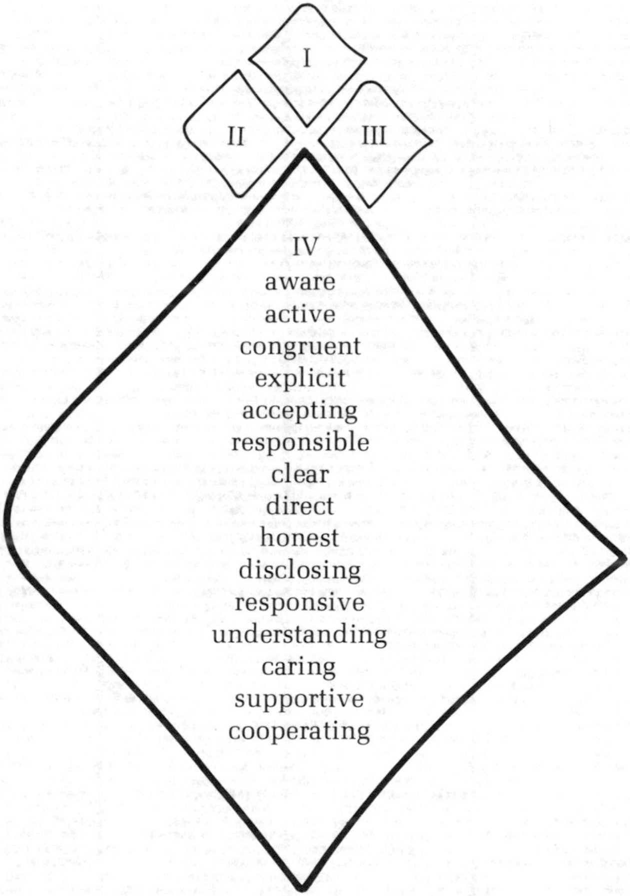

I

II   III

IV
aware
active
congruent
explicit
accepting
responsible
clear
direct
honest
disclosing
responsive
understanding
caring
supportive
cooperating

STYLE IV BEHAVIORS

Most of the behaviors involved in Style IV have been discussed in earlier chapters, so we will simply list these below without providing further examples. These behaviors are the ten skills and related processes discussed in the first two sections of the book. If you would like to review any of these, turn back to the appropriate chapters.

Self-Disclosure Skills:

1. Speaking for self
2. Making sense statements
3. Making interpretive statements

Process of
Documenting

4. Making feeling statements
5. Making intention statements
6. Making action statements

Awareness of Other Skills:

7. Checking out
8. Stating intention and asking for acknowledgment

Process of
Sharing
a Meaning

9. Acknowledging the sender's message
10. Confirming-clarifying

Additional Behaviors Associated with Style IV:

"Now" present time orientation:

"I'm feeling some uncertainty about what I just said."

"I'd like to stop talking about this now and come back to it later tonight."

Focus on self contribution/response:

"It's hard for me to understand your feelings, but I won't overlook them."

"I'm avoiding the issue because I'm scared."

"When you seriously consider what I want, I think you care a lot about me and I really feel happy."

A significant characteristic of Style IV behavior is completeness. You do not use just one or two skills, you use all of them. You do not disclose just one or two dimensions of the Awareness Wheel, you disclose all of them. This does not mean, however, that each Style IV statement includes all the different parts of the Awareness Wheel. It does mean that all of the dimensions pertaining to an issue are clearly and honestly disclosed during the conversation.

Our emphasis so far has been on completeness of self-disclosure in Style IV. Equally important are the skills for maintaining awareness of the other to support complete self-disclosure by your partner. Style IV behaviors not only serve the function of revealing your own Awareness Wheel to your partner, but also his/hers to you, thereby completing the relationship picture. Style IV promotes the sharing of each partner's self-awareness with the other; it promotes a two-way sharing process, not just one-way telling.

Using a style means not just how something is said; it is not just the language used; it is also the spirit (the intention) with which you say it. Effectively used, Style IV is accompanied by a spirit of nurturance, of helping yourself and your partner grow. Your tone of voice, the content of what you say, your body posture, your facial gestures all can be clues to the spirit behind what's being said. After you've experienced some Style IV communication, you will be able to know when you're in and out of it. There is a spirit of acceptance and a feeling of caring for self and partner that is unmistakable.

Let's look at another conversation to see how a Style IV conversation looks when all the skills are used and fit together. This is an actual verbatim tape transcription of two young people in their early twenties continuing to deal with an important issue in their lives.

Debbie: "Some time ago we talked to each other about where our relationship was going. We decided that we'd live together for awhile. I've been doing some thinking about it, and I don't want to just live together. I want to get married.

"I know I can anticipate how I'd feel living together. I'd have guilt. I wouldn't be able to handle it with my folks, especially since they live so close and I guess that's not really what I want at all anyhow. I'm willing to continue the relationship as it is, but when we decide to make a committed relationship, I want it committed in marriage."

Eric: "I want us to live together before we marry. Some day I do want to marry you but I also would like to live with you first. I guess partially it's because I've always wanted to do that, but I'd also like to see how I adjust to a really close 24-hour-a-day contact with my mate; with you. I'd like to try it out before I do it just to see that I'm sure. I think I know a lot of how it would be because we've spent an awful lot of time just staying at either one or the other's apartments. There's another thing, too. I really enjoy being single, and I enjoy being free and you know about that. I also hear how you'd feel with your parents. Your parents would be kind of upset if we were to live together; but I mainly hear you want our relationship to be committed."

Debbie: "It is really scary for me to talk to you like this because when we first started seeing each other you told me about several girls you started dating, and when they started getting into anything heavy, you ran. But I guess I have to stand where I am and say that I do want marriage or no living together. I won't live with you, and I get mad at your fear of committing yourself. I get mad because I want to change you and I want to say to you 'Hey, why don't you risk enough to get into it?' And sometimes I really get angry when I think you take such teeny steps towards risking any relationship. What do you hear me saying?"

Eric: "I'm very cautious and I progress very slowly toward a certain goal. Am I reading you right?"

Debbie: "No, not so much that as I get angry at how scared you are to make a commitment. You want to make a test case out of us living together first—you know, test it out and if it's cool, then okay, we'll make the final step. I guess I'm willing to risk that right away."

> Eric: "Okay. I guess I'm just not ready yet to risk that much—but you want to take the final risk? Am I hearing you correctly in that you're saying you don't want to just live with me; you want to be married to me?"
>
> Debbie: "Yes."

In this exchange, Eric and Debbie use all the skills and processes for sending clear, complete, and congruent messages. No resolution occurred. They're in the midst of the process of dealing with this crucial issue, and at this point the outcome is uncertain. What they have accomplished thus far is to focus their awareness and increase their understanding of themselves and each other.

In time, if they both stay in touch with their awareness, a resolution which is congruent for each of them will probably emerge. That's because self-awareness is an on-going process. Your sensations, ideas, feelings, wants, and actions are continually emerging as situations develop. Consequently, on-going self-awareness creates new issues and leads to the resolution of old ones. Each issue is unique, depending on the situation and persons involved. This is the reason it is impossible to effectively deal with issues by forcefully superimposing solutions. Solutions grow out of understanding and accepting on-going self-awareness. The process of dialogue around each issue contains its own unique solution when the process is complete and congruent.

Often solutions to issues don't come easily or immediately. At these times, forcing a solution will bring incongruent preclosure to the issue. Rather than preclosing, we think you are better off to wait and stay with your awareness, returning again to the issue with your partner as new awareness emerges and time passes. At other times, you may develop a solution which you and your partner aren't sure will be satisfactory. At these times it's useful to go ahead and act, but also use your Awareness Wheel to evaluate the impact of the action you have taken.

If closing things off too quickly is one danger, then never taking action is yet another one. Not taking action may indicate that you're deluding yourself into believing that you're really working on things when all that you're actually doing is "blocking" or going through the motions of working on an issue.

Admittedly there is a dilemma here. Trying to avoid premature closures yet maintaining a committment to do something about the issue—that's not easy. Our experience indicates that "workable plans for action" emerge after both you and your partner's self-disclosures are complete and both of you experience understanding. But keep in mind: sometimes taking action is not necessarily important. Often the processes of disclosing and being understood are the actions that really build the relationship.

What you eventually decide to do or not to do is your choice. Ready-made solutions from us or anyone else probably won't work for you. We think you are your own best inventor. This is where your personal choice and responsibility become paramount. However, we think you'll find that if you or your partner do not actively attend to process in your relationship, issues will continue unresolved, or occasionally they will resolve themselves by chance. Research suggests that partners in viable relationships develop their own techniques for responding early and effectively to issues rather than avoiding and neglecting them.[1] So deal with issues as they arise, and try to stay in Style IV to facilitate your own and your partner's self-disclosure. When you do this, you'll find yourselves attending to process and developing creative resolutions of issues.

SUMMARY OF STYLES

Styles vary in terms of both the intentions that are typically expressed and the specific behaviors used. Lists of the typical intentions and behaviors are contained in the various figures in the previous chapter and in this one. A summary of the intentions associated with each style is shown in Figure 9-2.

You'll note that we have supplied labels to the two diagonal dimensions. The dimensions of the upper right side of the diagram are labeled "disclosure/receptivity." Styles I and II are low in both self-disclosure and receptivity to partner's disclosures. A quick glance at the intentions listed under Styles I and II will show you that these styles simply do not disclose much of your own

[1]Jerry M. Lewis, John T. Gossett, and Virginia Austin Phillips, "A Research Study of Healthy Families," *The Journal of the National Association of Private Psychiatric Hospitals,* 3, No. I, (Spring 1971): 20-23.

Figure 9-2: Intentions Associated with Each Style

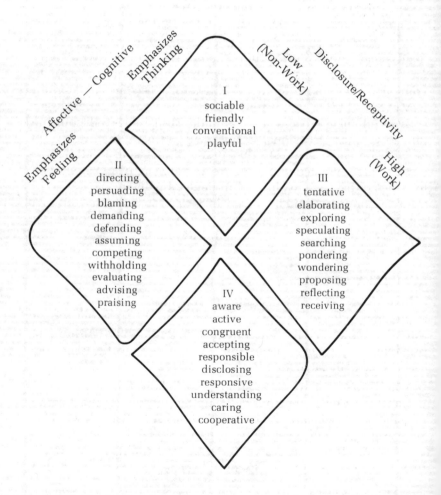

Awareness Wheel, and they don't encourage your partner to disclose his/hers either. On the other hand, the intentions listed under Styles III and IV do both of these things, especially Style IV.

The dimension on the upper left is labeled "affective — cognitive." Again, a glance at the intentions listed under Styles II and IV indicate that feelings are present with these styles. In Style IV feelings are expressed and acted on clearly and directly, whereas in Style II, they are more often concealed and acted out in a variety of indirect ways. But emotion is an important part of the messages sent with both styles. Style I and III messages, on the other hand, are typically low in emotion content. More often, they simply involve cognitive content—descriptions and ideas.

Because Styles III and IV are relatively high in self-disclosure and receptivity, we think of them as "work" styles, that is, styles which help zero in on personal and relationship issues. Both styles are useful in getting out the self-information necessary for dealing directly with issues. But since Style III is rather devoid of emotion, it is less likely than Style IV to probe the feelings and emotional depth often involved in issues. As a consequence, Style III is somewhat tentative and exploratory. Style IV, on the other hand, expresses a deeper commitment to deal with the issue. For this reason, we call Style III a *tentative work style* and Style IV a *committed work style*.

Lists of key words and typical behaviors which signal a particular style have also been presented in the previous chapter and in this one. A summary of the behaviors characteristic of each style is shown in Figure 9-3.

By now, you've probably concluded we think Style IV is a pretty important style. If so, you're absolutely right. We think Style IV is best when you and your partner have an issue and want to work on it. But we do not think that Style IV is the "best" style for communicating in all circumstances. Rather, as with any style, Style IV has inappropriate uses, too. It's all a matter of your intentions.

If your intention is to socialize and participate in some activities together, Style IV is too heavy. Style I would be better here. If your intention is to direct and persuade, then Style IV doesn't fit. Try Style II. If your intention is to explore tentatively and get a general

Figure 9-3: Behaviors Characteristic of each style.

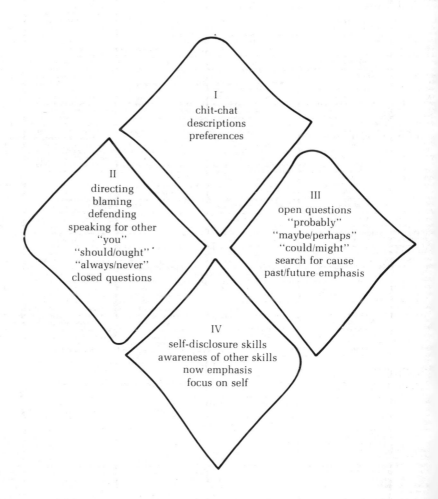

overview of an issue, then Style IV is too focused. Style III is better for that.

In short, each style plays an important role in effective and flexible interpersonal communication. Nevertheless, we have two major reasons for highlighting Style IV communication. First, most people learn how to use Style I and II as they grow up. Style III is often learned as a speculative, "intellectual" style if a person goes to college. Style IV is most often missing in a person's communication repertoire. So Style IV is important to round out your ability to communicate effectively. Secondly, we are convinced from our research and experience, that Style IV is the most effective way to deal with relationship issues.

These points bring us to the conclusion of our discussion of communication styles. In closing, we'd like to emphasize again that an effective communicator is flexible. She/he recognizes the differences in styles, can monitor his/her own style of communication, and is able to use different styles to appropriately express different intentions. No single style can be used to effectively communicate all the different intentions a person has. A flexible, effective communicator understands this and matches style with intentions. Before moving on to the discussion of mixed messages, we'd like you to pause for a moment and think about your own communication again. Are you basically a one or two style communicator, or do you use all of them? When do you typically use the various styles—I, II, III, and IV? Where do you use them, and with whom?

CHAPTER TEN

MIXED MESSAGES

In the last two chapters, we've presented a framework for thinking about alternative verbal communication styles. In this chapter, we're going to add an element to complete this framework. But before doing this, we'd like to discuss the reasons we've presented the Communication Styles Framework.

The basic purpose for presenting the framework is to help you understand several important aspects of verbal communication. We've emphasized two main points in our discussion. First, we've described at some length and provided numerous examples of the different behaviors people use when they communicate. Second, we've looked carefully at the relationship between the intentions people have and the behaviors they use to express these intentions. So basically what we've been trying to do is help you become more sensitive to stylistic variation; to differences in ways people communicate.

Our purpose then has been to *describe* how people communicate; not to *prescribe* how you should communicate. In fact, we think you'll find that your communication becomes stiff and stilted, losing much of its spontaneity, if you purposely try to talk in particular styles. When you are able to use all the styles, though, your communication can become more flexible. The way to increase your flexibility is not to consciously try to use different styles, but rather, to focus on learning and using alternative skills. And try to use those skills which effectively express your intentions. If you focus on the skills, you will find yourself using the various styles effectively.

MIXED MESSAGES

One thing we'd like you to recognize about the Verbal Communication Styles Framework is that it isn't a completely accurate description of communication styles. The four styles we've described are "pure" styles in the sense of involving clear intentions and specific types of behavior. However, more often than not, messages are not pure examples of a particular style. Rather, they tend to be mixed. *Messages become mixed when any intention or behavior from Style II slips into another style.* One part of the message is "straight" (Style I, III, or IV), but the second part is an added undercurrent which usually contradicts the straight part (Style II). Often mixed messages grow out of your *incomplete* or *incongruent* self-awareness. And they often communicate tension—tension inside yourself or tension between you and your partner. Let's look at some examples of mixed messages:

"You're such a cute jerk." (Style I mixed tone and laughter suggest play, but label suggests a hidden message.)

"Sometimes you almost make me feel wanted." (Style I mixed: tone suggests playful joking positive message—words suggest uncertainty and giving to the other responsibility for self's experience.)

"I don't understand why you don't listen to me." (Style III mixed with blame and closed assumption.)

"I mean, for once, she didn't have to blame me, because you did it—not me." (Style III mixed: clarifying meaning with a bit of self put-down and blame of other.)

"It pleases me that you take stuff from the kids and it doesn't upset you." (Style IV mixed—A positive message about other with two closed assumptions.)

"I feel excited about my stopping smoking; now you should too." (Style IV mixed: clear feeling and action statement about self with condition for other.)

There are two major reasons why mixed messages occur: First, strong feelings are aroused but are not reported. This most often happens when a couple is discussing something in the line of a "there-and-then" topic about which some immediate "here-and-now" feelings are stirred up and not reported directly. Second, intentions become mixed and only certain of the intentions are reported directly. When the undisclosed intentions are of a Style II type—to persuade, blame, control, or change your partner—these result in a Style II message mixing in with and contaminating your Style I, III, or IV messages.

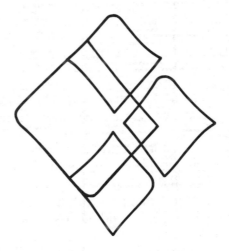

This is not unusual, of course, because it's hard to always be immediately in touch with your feelings, and we often have multiple intentions in a situation. Our messages come out as mixed when we express these feelings and multiple intentions *indirectly*. Mixed messages can be reduced in number—even if not eliminated entirely—by keeping tuned in to your immediate feelings and intentions and disclosing these directly. Let's look at how the earlier examples of mixed messages might sound if they were sent as straight messages, disclosing feelings and intentions directly.

"I think you were off base there, but I'm not really sore, just a little irritated. Anyway, I think you're cute."

"I'd like to feel wanted more than I do, but I don't want to make a federal case out of it, either. I'm inclined to think it may be the way I see myself rather than something between us. Just the same, I'd like to hear about your appreciation for me when you feel it."

"I get burned up when I don't think you're listening to me. I just asked a question, and I didn't hear you say anything."

"I feel relieved that she didn't tie into me. I have to admit I even feel kind of glad it was you who did it and not me."

"I really enjoy watching how you handle the kids. You don't appear to lose your cool even when they come at you with all kinds of stuff."

"I feel excited about my stopping smoking. I wish you'd stop, too. I think it would be better for you."

How to Identify Mixed Messages.

There are a number of behavioral clues to mixed messages. Several vocal characteristics are important clues, such as a harsh voice quality, whiny, sarcastic, or demanding tone of voice. Facial expressions that don't match the thought or feeling being expressed are also significant, such as a smile or grin with a complaint, or a look of anger with a soft, supportive statement.

Verbal combinations indicate mixed messages, too. Particularly important here are the parts of the message that are emphasized. For example, many people send blaming messages in a subtle way by prefacing their "you" statements with "I":

"I think *you* do this to me because you delight in getting me mad."

"I wonder why *you're* so selfish."

Here, the "you" parts of the message are expressing *closed assumptions* the speaker has about his partner—"You like to make me mad," "you're selfish." Other word clues to closed assumptions that produce mixed messages are, "never," "always," "every time," etc.

"But I think you always do it!"

Another type of statement indicating a closed assumption and a mixed message comes in question form. Typically, the intention to persuade causes the mixing:

> "I'm wondering why you don't want to do it my way?" (Style III mixed.)
>
> "Could it be that you don't think . . .?" (Style III mixed.)
>
> "I like you 'cause you're so different." (Style I mixed said as a joke; or Style IV mixed said seriously with closed assumption.)

A different type of mixed message that usually involves an intention to persuade, too, is the "yes, but." The speaker appears to agree with his partner, but adds his own persuasive message:

> *Mary:* "I don't really think we can take a vacation and fix up the basement this year without borrowing money."
>
> *Bill:* "Well, I certainly agree that we're a little short on cash now, and it might not be possible to do both, but I think we'll be able to work it out with some good planning; in fact, I'm sure we can."

A final common mixed message is one involving build-up and put-down words together. The intention causing the mix here isn't usually persuasion; rather, it's an intention to blame, label, or hurt.

> "I really appreciate your interest and your concern for me, but you're so darn demanding."
>
> "I think you're awfully attractive and enjoy being with you if only you weren't so flighty."

Coping with Mixed Messages.

The problem with mixed messages is that they are confusing to your partner. Which part should he/she respond to—the "straight" part or the hidden, Style II part? Preliminary indications in our research indicate that most people respond to the hidden part. About a third of the time, they respond directly with a Style II message of their own, for example, by responding to a hidden persuasion attempt by resisting, or by counter-attacking when they have been subtly blamed or labeled. In most other instances, their response involves a mixed message in return, typically resulting in an extended cycle of mixed messages.

As a receiver, it's not necessary to fire back with either a Style II message or a mixed message. You do have other choices. One thing you can do is try to split up the message, acknowledging both the "straight" part and the hidden part, and asking for clarification.

> John: "I wonder how come you're not interested in what I have to say?"
>
> Mary: "Hey, wait a minute! I hear you saying I'm not listening to you, but I also hear you jumping to the conclusion that I don't care much about you. Can you straighten out that message for me?"

Another way to deal with mixed messages as a receiver is to acknowledge both parts of the message, then clearly indicate which part you are responding to.

> Joan: "I feel upset when you never want to do anything I enjoy doing."
>
> Mark: "Just a second. I hear a 'you never' in there and I'm getting sore. I'd like to tune in to what's bothering you, but I'm finding it hard to hear anything but the 'you never' part."

As a sender, if you find yourself slipping into mixed messages when you don't want to, look at your intentions and be aware of your feelings. Is your Style II intention the primary one, or is the intention tied in with the other style the more important one? If one intention is primary, try to express it clearly and directly. If your intentions really are mixed then try to express all of them clearly and directly, acknowledging that you do have mixed intentions. Look at this subtle mixed message:

> "I like it when you take the initiative and make arrangements for some of the fun things we do together, like going to that play last night. I really appreciated that, and I hope I can rely on you for that."

Here the speaker is expressing appreciation for the partner's effort, but also indirectly asking partner to continue doing it. Straightened out, this message might sound like this:

> "I'm glad you took responsibility for making those arrangements last night. I don't like to. I'd really like it if you would do that most of the time. Would you be willing to?"

Figure 10-1 illustrates how mixed messages fit into the Verbal Communication Styles Framework.

Figure 10-1. Mixed Messages.

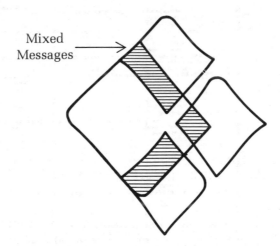

Mixed
Messages

Although we have been emphasizing ways to cope with and clarify mixed messages, we don't want to suggest that you will be able to avoid them entirely. They're quite natural in our everyday language. But when you want to be clear and promote understanding with your partner, try to avoid mixed messages. Communication becomes clearer the "straighter" the style is. The best way to send straight messages is to look closely at your feelings and intentions and use the skills which express them most clearly. If necessary, acknowledge your mixed feelings and multiple intentions and disclose them directly.

KEY IDEAS FROM SECTION III

1. Styles of communication are determined by intentions and behaviors.

2. Four communication styles can be identified.

3. Styles I and II are nonwork styles; Styles III and IV are work styles.

4. Style IV discloses complete and congruent self-awareness and is open to partner's disclosures.

5. Style IV utilizes all of the self-disclosure and awareness-of-other skills.

6. Indirect, confusing mixed messages happen when Style II is mixed with other styles.

PATTERNS OF COMMUNICATION

The emphasis in the first three sections has been on basic skills and principles for increasing your effectiveness as a communicator. We have identified three keys for becoming a skilled communicator:

1. Maintain self-awareness and use the self-disclosure skills to reveal it completely and congruently to your partner.

2. Use awareness-of-others skills to help your partner disclose his/her self-awareness.

3. Use different styles when you have different intentions to express—be a flexible communicator.

All of these will help you become a better communicator. But to use communication effectively to build your relationship requires several more things. That's what the chapters in Section IV are about.

Besides skills, the "spirit" of interaction with your partner determines how effective the two of you will be in building your relationship. The "I count/I count you" orientation discussed in Chapter 11, expresses the essential spirit for relationship building.

A second requirement for building relationships is that partners work directly on issues arising in their partnership. Avoidance of issues results in no growth. Dealing with issues directly and effectively can result in relationship development. The "mini-contract" will help you do this. It is described in Chapter 12.

Lastly, as you use communication to build your relationship, it's important to know what to do when your interaction gets off the track. Chapter 13 helps you to learn how to "trouble shoot" your communication.

CHAPTER ELEVEN

BUILDING SELF AND OTHER ESTEEM

Each of us has a mental "picture" of him/herself. If you look closely, you find that it's not a single picture. Rather, it includes both snapshots and movies of yourself alone and yourself interacting with others—from time past, present, and the imagined future. You'll probably note some variety in the scenes: Depending on time, place, situation, who you're with, you're somewhat different. But some attributes seem to stand out more than others. And some patterns of action seem to be repeated more than others. Held at arm's length, the collage seems to meld into a single impression; we refer to this image as our "self-concept."

Accompanying this picture of yourself is an accumulated set of evaluations and judgments: successful, unsuccessful, approval, disapproval, competent, incompetent, loving, unloving, and many more. Add to these an accumulated set of feelings about self: admiration, shame, confidence, warmth, hope, guilt, pleasure, etc. This set of evaluations, judgments, and feelings, comprise one's sense of self-worth, one's self-esteem. Some of these evaluations and feelings seem to predominate more than others, and we may speak of one person as having high self-esteem (approves and feels good about him/herself most of the time) and another as having low self-esteem (usually disapproves and feels bad about him/herself).

Thus, what we find for most people is a somewhat stable self-concept accompanied by a relatively stable sense of self-worth or self-esteem. People who are typically alive and aware with high self-esteem occasionally experience low esteem. However, when this occurs, it's usually a temporary circumstance and does not become an indicator of their over-all esteem position.

Your self-concept and your self-esteem affect what you see in situations and meanings you make, the feelings you experience, the intentions you entertain, and the actions you choose. And since you cannot *not* communicate, your evaluations and feelings about yourself are being communicated in your tone of voice, body posture, facial expressions, and gestures, as well as with the words you use. Your communication is constantly giving off clues about how you value yourself. This tends to influence how others value you, which in turn reinforces your original self-valuation, and so on *ad infinitum!* Let's look at contrasting examples of messages from two different people:

> *Bill:* (vibrant, buoyant manner) "I think I just had a good idea! Let me tell you about it!"
>
> *John:* (monotone, unenthusiastic) "I had an idea about that, not that it's anything special. Let me see if I can remember it now."

What kind of esteem messages is each of the two communicating about himself? And which of the two is more likely to receive close attention, i.e., a message back from the listener that says "I value what you have to say"? Let's take a look at another set of contrasting examples:

> *Liz:* (animated, enthusiastic) "The weather's perfect and I'd love to go to the beach! How about it . . . would you like to go with me?"
>
> *Delores:* (hesitant) "I don't suppose you'd care to go to the beach with me."

What message is each of these communicating about how she expects her intentions (desires) to be received? Who's more likely to end up at the beach?

At this point, we want to call attention to the association between self-concept, and self-esteem, and the five dimensions in your

Awareness Wheel. We have spoken of the self-concept as a remembered or inwardly-pictured set of sensory data (sensing dimension) and the self-esteem as an accumulated set of evaluations and judgments (interpreting dimension) and feelings (feeling dimension). If we stopped here, we might leave the impression that self-concept and self-esteem are determined and forever set by past events and your inner experience of these past events. This might leave you with the impression that there is little you can do about it *now*. But wait a moment! There are two more dimensions of awareness: intending and doing. This is the crucial point: *Your self-concept and self-esteem are not static structures but are names for dynamic processes involving all dimensions of awareness—including current intentions and actions.* How you picture yourself and how you value yourself are influenced by your intentions and by what you do about them. How you treat yourself, accept, and utilize your self-awareness in each situation affects your picture of yourself and either enhances or diminishes your self-esteem. You can *decide* and you can *act* in ways that say you value yourself or, "I count," or in ways which say you don't value yourself or, "I don't count."

A major factor in carrying out the decision that you count is your full acceptance of self-awareness—owning and attending to your own perceptions, impressions, feelings, intentions, and actions, whether they are painful or pleasurable. An experience of low self-esteem is more likely to be temporary for the person who fully attends to his awareness rather than denying it because complete self-awareness helps him to deal with the circumstances directly until he regains buoyancy and high esteem.

Your concept of others, your partner, your friends, and your evaluations of them are also somewhat stable in much the same manner as self-concept and self-esteem. Again, we wish to emphasize that this is a dynamic, on-going process. In each situation you can *decide* and you can *act* in ways that say you value the other—"I count you"—or in ways that say you don't value the other—"I don't count you." You can *choose*, and each choice makes a contribution to your concept of the other and your esteem of him/her.

Stop for a moment and recall a recent situation in which you valued your partner:

Where were you? (home, work, school, etc.?)

How did you feel?

What were you doing to express how he counted to you?

Each of us is involved—or has at some time been involved—in a relationship with another in which we think of the two of us together. Over time each of us develops a picture of "we." This "picture" is also a composite of many snapshots and movies of the two of us in action and interacting with others. The features which characterize the "we" may be similar to or quite different from the features characterizing my partner and me individually. For example, two partners in a relationship may be quite gregarious and sociable as individuals but when together rarely interact with other individuals or couples. Or two partners may perceive self and other as aggressive in their individual business or professional lives, but carry a picture of the two of them together as congenial and non competitive when they interact with others. Accompanying this picture of the "we" is an accumulated set of evaluations, judgments, and feelings about the picture, about "us." This makes up my esteem of the relationship. Just as with esteem of self and other, I can choose and I can act in ways which indicate that the relationship counts to me. I can act in ways which indicate that I discount the relationship. These decisions and actions will then influence how I picture the relationship system and how much I value it—again, a continuing dynamic process.

A major issue in many relationship systems revolves around the question of whether or not one partner or the other is giving high enough priority to the relationship. For instance, you probably know of a marriage in which one partner is devoting so much time and energy to business or profession that there is little left for the relationship.

Here we wanted only to bring to your attention the fact that you have a concept of and esteem for your relationship. In the remainder of this chapter we will focus on self-concept and self-esteem as they produce a sequence of pictures of your relationship. In developing pictures of your relationship we want you to become more aware of (1) how you *value* yourself and your partner, (2) how you *accept* your own and your partner's awareness, and (3) how you *communicate* your esteem by using your awareness.

INDIVIDUAL SELF/OTHER ESTEEM POSITIONS

Every situation I face involving an issue can be approached from a position of valuing myself or one of not valuing myself. We call these the two *self-esteem* positions: either I count myself or I don't count myself.[1]

I Count Myself.

I count myself when:

—I try to be completely and congruently "in contact with" my self-awareness: what I am sensing, thinking, feeling, wanting, doing.

—I accept my awareness of who I really am regardless of how difficult or painful this might be. I embrace rather than attempt to escape my awareness. I *own* my perceptions, thoughts, feelings, wants, and actions.

Since awareness is an on-going process, being in contact and fully accepting ownership of my awareness gives me an on-going basis for meeting and dealing with issues—creating and discovering solutions that are congruent rather than superimposing solutions that don't really fit (incongruent solutions).

Table 11-1 presents the typical self-awareness of someone who counts him/herself.

[1]Many of the ideas discussed in this chapter are extensions of concepts discussed by James Sorrells and Frederick Ford "Toward an Integrated Theory of Families and Family Therapy," *Psychotherapy: Theory, Research, and Practice*, Vol. 6, #3, 1969, pp. 150-160.

Table 11-1

AWARENESS AND ESTEEM. I COUNT MYSELF WHEN:

Sensing

—I permit full awareness of what I am seeing, hearing, touching, smelling, tasting.

—I own and respect my perceptions, whether or not these are different from those of other people.

—I own and respect my perceptions, whether they are pleasant or unpleasant.

Interpreting

—I'm aware of my own thoughts, conclusions, assumptions, evaluations, judgments.

—I own my judgments about myself, whether these be critical or appreciative.

—I value my self-judgments, critical or appreciative, regardless of whether these agree with those of other people.

—I remain open to the possibility of changing my opinions, assumptions, and judgments as new and different information is received.

Feeling

—I tune into my feelings, especially those about myself.

—I own and value these feelings, both the painful ones and the pleasant ones.

—I permit awareness of a full range of feelings and do not screen out "unacceptable" ones.

Intending

—I tune in to my intentions, especially those about myself— what I want for myself now *and* long-range.

—I permit awareness of my "unacceptable" intentions as well as those which I and others would approve.

—I own my intentions.

—I'm aware of contradictory intentions and aware of assigning priority to some wants over others.

Doing

—I pay attention to my actions.

—I'm aware of how my thoughts, feelings, and intentions are expressed in my actions.

—I make choices and own the decisions I make.

—I accept responsibility for what I do.

Besides maintaining and owning awareness, there are specific overt actions which we view as "I count" behavior. These include:

—contributing

—making decisions

—asking for and accepting help

—receiving love and affection

—taking and accepting responsibility for myself

—caring for myself

—enjoying myself

—honestly, clearly, and directly disclosing my thoughts, feelings, and wants.

I Don't Count Myself.

Now, let's look at the second self-esteem position from which you can approach a situation:

I don't count myself when:

—I'm out of touch with my self-awareness.

—I don't fully accept responsibility for and "own" my self-awareness.

When these things happen, I no longer have a reliable basis for meeting and dealing with issues. Table 11-2 represents the typical self-awareness of someone who does not count him/herself.

Table 11-2

AWARENESS AND ESTEEM. I DON'T COUNT MYSELF WHEN:

Sensing

   —I disregard what my senses tell me.

   —I permit awareness of only certain kinds of data, for example, screening out what I saw or heard if it is "unacceptable."

   —I own and respect my perceptions only if these agree with other peoples' perceptions; in short, I mistrust my perceptions.

Interpreting

   —I pay little attention to my own thoughts, conclusions, assumptions, evaluations, judgments.

   —I disown my self-critical judgments, and my self-appreciative judgments.

   —I value my thoughts, conclusions, assumptions, evaluations, or judgments only when they agree with those of others.

   —I do not permit myself to change my mind.

Feeling

   —I pay little attention to my feelings (especially about myself).

   —I don't own my feelings but attribute ownership and responsibility to others.

   —I permit awareness of only certain kinds of feelings about myself.

Intending

   —I do not tune in to my intentions for myself.

   —I fail to accept responsibility for what I want for myself.

   —I screen "unacceptable" wants from my awareness.

   —I don't permit awareness of contradictory or incompatible wants.

Doing

 —I'm not aware of what I'm doing.

 —I do not pay attention to how my thoughts, feelings, and intentions are being expressed in my actions.

 —I'm not aware of choosing, and I disown the decisions I make.

 —I do not own my actions but rather view myself as merely directed by others or by outside events.

Besides failing to maintain and own your self-awareness, there are specific overt actions which we view as "I don't count" behavior. These include:

 —putting myself down

 —placating

 —sulking

 —procrastinating

 —refusing love and affection

 —not accepting honest admiration expressed by others

 —not asking for and not accepting help

 —avoiding responsibility for self

 —failing to provide self-care

 —evaluating my own efforts purely on the basis of *outcome* and ignoring the creativity, joy, pain, and learning associated with the *process* of moving toward an objective

Stop for a moment and recall a recent situation in which you did not count yourself:

 Where were you? (home, work, school, etc.)

 Who were you with? (partner, friend, alone, etc.)

 What were you doing to express your not-counting?

 How did you feel?

Similarly, when I face a situation involving an issue, I can approach it from a position of valuing my partner or not valuing him/her. We call these *other-esteem* positions: "I count you or I don't count you."

I Count You.

I count you when:

—I pay attention to you, to your expressions of your awareness, and I maintain and own my awareness of you.

—I respect and trust your self-disclosure as a report of your self-awareness, even if I don't like what I hear.

Being in contact with you and accepting your awareness "as it is" gives me a basis for dealing with our issues—creating and discovering congruent solutions rather than superimposing incongruent ones. Table 11-3 represents the typical self-awareness of someone who counts the other person.

Table 11-3

AWARENESS AND ESTEEM. I COUNT YOU WHEN:

Sensing

—I pay attention to sensory data from you and about you—what I see, hear, touch, taste, smell.

—I accept the data my senses receive about you.

Interpreting

—I permit myself to be aware of your full range of qualities and capabilities, both those which I like and those I dislike.

—I own my evaluations and judgments about you, both positive and critical ones.

—I do not dwell on my critical evaluations of you or screen out my positive judgments when I'm angry with you.

Feeling

—I tune in to my feelings toward you—love, anger, trust, admiration, contempt—whatever these may be.

—I fully own these feelings toward you as mine and accept responsibility for them.

—I respect your feelings as belonging to you.

Intending

—I tune into my intentions for you—to what I want from you and what I want for you.

—I accept responsibility for my intentions toward you.

—I maintain awareness of your intentions as disclosed by you.

—I'm aware that you are responsible for what you want.

Doing

—I permit awareness of what I'm doing in relation to you, how my thoughts, feelings, and intentions toward you are being expressed through my action.

—I accept full responsibility for my own actions toward you.

—I'm aware that you own and are responsible for what you do.

—I tune in to the impact of my actions upon you and to the impact of your actions upon me.

Besides maintaining and owning my awareness of other, there are specific overt actions which we view as "I count you" behavior. These include:

—checking out my assumptions about your thoughts, feelings, and wants

—letting you know "where I'm coming from" (disclosing my self-awareness about you)

—working toward understanding rather than controlling

—leaving room for, and even appreciating our differences

—providing feedback that can be useful to you, both positive and negative (specific descriptive information regarding behavior over which you have control, disclosed to you at a time when you may be ready to hear it)

—avoiding taking and accepting responsibility for you

—giving help

—cooperating with you in mutual tasks, in problem-solving, and in relationship building activities

—refraining from putting you down (especially in front of others or behind your back)

—sharing in fun activities and enjoying you

I Don't Count You.

The second other-esteem position from which you may approach a situation is the "I don't count you" position. I don't count you when:

—I do not pay attention to you, to your expressions of your awareness, and I do not maintain and own my awareness of you.

—I refuse to accept and believe your self-disclosure as a report of your true awareness.

A result of these things is that I don't have a reliable basis for working with you toward congruent solutions to our issues. Table 11-4 represents the typical awareness of someone who does not count the other person.

Table 11-4

AWARENESS AND ESTEEM. I DON'T COUNT YOU WHEN:

Sensing

—I pay little attention to sensory data from you and about you—what I see, hear, touch, taste, smell.

—I screen out important data my senses receive about you.

Interpreting

—I permit awareness of only a narrow range of evaluations and judgments which I make about you.

—I fail to tune in to what you reveal about your thoughts, conclusions, assumptions, evaluations, judgments.

—When I'm angry at you, I dwell on my critical evaluations of you and screen from awareness my appreciative and positive evaluations.

Feeling

—I do not tune in to my feelings toward you.

—I do not own my feelings toward you but rather attribute responsibility to you for my feelings.

—I assume responsibility for your feelings.

Intending

—I fail to tune in to my intentions toward you—to what I want from you and what I want for you.

—I hold you responsbile for my intentions toward you.

—I do not maintain awareness of your intentions as disclosed by you.

—I presume to be responsible for what you want.

Doing

—I fail to maintain my awareness of what I'm doing in relation to you, what intentions and feelings I'm expressing through my actions.

—I hold you responsible for my actions toward you.

—I presume to be responsbile for what you do.

—I do not tune in to the impact of my actions on you or to the impact of your actions on me.

Here are some specific overt actions which we view as "I don't count you" behavior:

—rather than asking, I assume that I know what you think, feel, and want

—failing to let you know where I'm coming from (failing to self-disclose)

—working towards controlling rather than understanding

—attempting to manipulate or force change in you

—forcing agreement

—taking or accepting responsibility for you

—withholding help

—competing rather than cooperating

—putting you down with ridicule, sarcasm, ignoring, or disregarding

—providing non useful feedback (poorly timed; labels rather than description; focusing on something over which you have no control)

—concentrating on your "liabilities" rather than your "assets"

—withholding my enjoyment of you

Stop for a moment and recall a recent situation in which you did not count the other:

Where were you? (home, work, school, etc.)

Who were you with? (partner, friend, colleague, etc.)

What were you doing to express your not-counting to the other?

How did you feel?

COMBINING SELF-OTHER ESTEEM POSITIONS

The messages you send reflect what's inside of you—how you value yourself and your partner. How you choose to deal with an issue from an esteem point of view depends on what your intention is toward yourself and your partner—to count or not to count yourself and your partner. At any one time you can combine one of the two *self-esteem* positions with one of the two *other-esteem* positions to form a basic *self-other orientation* to the situation. There are four possible combinations. Let's examine each of these.

I Don't Count/I Don't Count You.

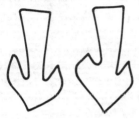

Here, when there's an issue, I treat both of us as being not very worthwhile. I may act this way because I am out of contact with my own awareness or fail to fully own my awareness and because I pay little attention to my partner's messages or don't trust my partner's disclosures. This combination is characterized by feelings of hopelessness and despair, because I am acting as if neither one of us can take charge of him/herself and direct his/her own course of action responsibly.

My messages may contain direct put-downs of both myself and my partner (Style II); or I may devalue myself and my partner in an indirect way, for example, with noncommittal or irrelevant topics and messages (Style I or III). I may give the impression that I'm leaving our destiny to chance or hoping for some outside authority to give us direction. Let's look at an example:

> "I can't be any different from the way I am! You're lucky to have done this well!" (Translated: I am unable to take care of myself, you are not worth much either.)

In the example above, painful feelings about self and angry feelings toward partner are not directly and explicitly expressed—possibly because the speaker is not fully in touch with them, or because s/he has no hope that s/he can change. Instead feelings are acted out in a manner that puts both partners down (Style II). Here's another example:

> *Laura:* "Say, is something bugging you? You didn't answer when I asked you if you want french toast or pancakes. In fact, I haven't heard a word from you since you woke up. I'm feeling left out."
>
> *Ron:* "Let's have pancakes. Okay?"

Ron ignores the relationship message in Laura's statement, as he attempts to come back with a Style I "smooth it over and keep it conversational" sort of reply. Possibly Ron didn't want to get into anything "heavy," but if this was the case, he failed to state this intention directly. Again, the reason may have been that he was not tuned in to his own feelings and intentions or failed to accept ownership of them. Let's look at one more example:

> *Steve:* "I'm feeling angry right now 'cause I don't think you really tried to understand what I'm saying."
>
> *Donna:* "That's possible; it seems to be a common pattern."

Donna probably had some strong feelings as she heard Steve's Style IV statement, but her response in Style III was inappropriate to the seriousness of the issue and the intensity of feelings. As a consequence, Donna is putting both herself and Steve down.

Of course, when Style I and Style III are misused, as in the examples above, they are not true Style I or Style III messages but rather are examples of mixed messages, I/II and III/II. The *words* may sound straight Style I or Style III, but the hidden intentions add an undercurrent of tension that produces incongruent communication.

I Count/I Don't Count You.

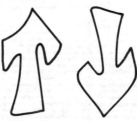

When you find yourself in this orientation, it's very likely because you've defined the situation as one in which one is right/the other wrong, or one wins/the other loses. In effect, you are saying, "Since only one of us can be valued in this situation, *I'll* be the one!" You're probably engaged in trying to control and dominate the outcome of the situation at the expense of both your partner and the relationship. You overemphasize your own perceptions, opinions, wants, feelings, and actions, and underemphasize or pay little attention to those of your partner.

This orientation is usually expressed with Style II—labeling, blaming, demanding, or threatening, and defense of self. These Style II messages frequently elicit similar responses from your partner. Most quarrels are characterized by I count/I don't count you intention sets enacted by *both* partners.

> *Jerry:* "Why in the heck did you say that in front of my brother? I'm not that way, and you know he'll use that against me some time. You sure are dumb!"
>
> *Karen:* "I said it 'cause it's true. If you don't want me to say things like that, you should change yourself. Or maybe you're not strong enough to change."

In this short dialogue, both Jerry and Karen are labeling the other, demanding something from the other, and claiming that "I am right." It's pretty obvious they are not going to get very far in resolving the issue; in fact, they probably won't even be able to identify what it is.

Actually, there seems to be a fallacy inherent in the I count/I don't count you position. The fallacy is that I can count myself and not count my partner. It's a fallacy because when you put your partner down, you're devaluing your relationship. You are saying in effect, "I'm involved in a worthless relationship." But since worthwhile people don't put their time and energy into worthless relationships, you discount yourself in the process of discounting your partner. So the I count/I don't count you position is a tenuous one at best, and ultimately dissolves into the more fundamental position of I don't count/I don't count you.

I Don't Count/I Count You.

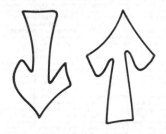

In this orientation, I depreciate myself while attempting to please and placate you. I devalue myself and (seemingly) value you. I may even appear as a martyr, sacrificing my good for your good. In this position, you're right, I'm wrong; you're important, I'm not important. I pay attention to your thoughts, feelings, and wants, and fail to attend to my own. I may use a direct Style II to depreciate myself and affirm you, but more often in this set one finds mixed Styles I/II or III/II.

> Lois: "I'm concerned about how we make decisions sometimes. Like last night when we were talking about getting a new car. I thought both of us were feeling very frustrated because we couldn't seem to get a handle on how we might reduce our expenses so we could pay for it. But then you just kind of blew up, stomped around, and so on. I was very angry at you. I don't think we can make decisions if that happens. I'd like to talk about what we might do differently."

> Larry: "Well you're right and I'm really sorry about it. I get so frustrated, I just lose control. I can't seem to stop myself from doing this. Maybe it would be better if you just made these decisions. You know you make good decisions and this would keep these bad situations from happening."

Here Larry uses a Style III/II to put himself down and, at the same time, build Lois up. But he does so in such a way that he tries to shift responsibility to Lois for both making the decisions and keeping himself from blowing up. How do you suppose Lois would feel about that?

Adopting the I don't count/I count you orientation involves a contradiction, however. When you do this, you really discount your partner. For example, when I demean myself and try to shift responsibility to my partner, as Larry did, I fail to count my partner's right to *not* be responsible for me. It's almost as if I'm saying, "You have no choice; you've got to take care of me." And when I try to take away my partner's choice, I discount him/her. When I behave in a placating way towards my partner, I convey that my partner is too fragile, unstable, or mean for me to level with—and discount him/her in that way. Or if I act the martyr, I convey a message that my partner welcomes my demeaning myself—implying that my partner doesn't care about me much. The next time someone behaves toward you in a demeaning, placating, or martyring way, be aware of your feeling response. You'll probably feel annoyed or irritated. These are predictable feeling responses when you receive a subtle putdown.

A special hazard in communicating I don't count/I count you resides in the likelihood of the other agreeing with me and responding with messages that say "you're right—you really don't count." Of course, this won't help my self-esteem any. Another hazard is that my partner may be lured into a game of "rescuing" my self-esteem. But s/he will probably resent being "used" in this fashion, and this sure won't help in building our relationship! Just as with the I count/I don't count you orientation, ultimately the I don't count/I count you position resolves into the position of I don't count/I don't count you, too!

The three orientations described so far all have in common the effect of preventing you and your partner from talking congruently with each other because:

—they interfere with your getting down to brass tacks around important issues, either directly or indirectly;

—they fail to convey respect and fail to acknowledge awareness of self and awareness of partner;

—if you attempt to count only one partner—you *or* your partner—your objective is to manipulate rather than understand.

In an intimate relationship it's impossible to really count yourself or your partner without counting *both*.

I Count/I Count You—We Both Count.

In this orientation, you are tuned in to self and accept your awareness. And you are also alert to your partner and trust your partner's self-disclosures. You value both yourself and your partner. You demonstrate commitment to your own well-being and growth and to your partner's well-being and growth as well. If your partner at the same time is acting on intentions to count self and other, then together you can face issues and conflicts directly with confidence, and you can find solutions congruent for both of you. The two of you are not leaving your destiny to chance. You experience hope that you can work things out together. Your relationship is characterized by "we both are important and together we can work things out."

You will be using Style IV, or Styles IV and III in combination, when you are sending I count/I count you messages while dealing with a meaningful issue.

> *Diane:* "We'd really like you and Jim to come over for a barbecue, and see our new house. It's really nice. Could you come this weekend?"
>
> *Lynn:* "Sounds like you're really excited about your new house, Diane, and I'd like to come over and see it. Exams start next week so Jim and I can't give you a definite time until we are through with them. I'll call you as soon as they are done to arrange a time. Would that be okay?"

Here Lynn turns down Diane's invitation, but does so in a way which acknowledges Diane's feelings about her house and also her own commitments to school. Then she makes a future action statement indicating a definite intention to follow through. In these ways she is counting both herself and Diane.

When there is not an issue, I count/I count you is expressed in play or in sociable "rapping" or chit-chat—or sometimes in Style IV, positive intimate enjoyment. And sometimes, positive, spontaneous Style II statements also have their way of saying I count/I count you—such as "We're great!" with lots of affection.

SKILLS FOR BUILDING SELF AND OTHER ESTEEM

"Both count" messages can be hard to send, especially when you and your partner disagree. In a disagreement, there's a temptation to shift from an intention to understand to an intention to win. If acted upon, the intention to win leads to an I count/I don't count you orientation, usually expressed with Style II or with mixed messages. To maintain an I count/I count you position, all of the skills we've presented earlier in the book are relevant and helpful. It's not just what I say (content) that indicates counting self and other but how I go about it (process). For example, documenting impressions or conclusions with sensory data requires real effort on my part; an effort to put you in the picture which says to your partner, "You count to me." And asking partner to reflect back my message says that I treat both my message and your understanding of it as important—we both count.

Both count messages also are hard to send when you're feeling hurt or angry. At such times communication skills can help you to keep clear of messages which blame, defend, or demand change in your partner. A clear commitment to the I count/I count you position and a lot of communication skill is needed to approach differences with the intention to understand and reconcile rather than to assign blame. It's especially important to keep tuned in to your intentions:

—What do you want for yourself, immediately, and long range?

—What do you want for your partner, immediately, and long range?

—What do you want for your relationship, immediately, and long range?

In any situation, both you and your partner can act from any one of four possible orientations towards self and other. Since each of you has four orientations to choose from, four times four means your relationship can be characterized by any one of *sixteen* different pictures! With all these possibilities, it's easy to see why it would be difficult to maintain a mutual I count/I count you relationship, especially around a conflict issue or disagreement. This is exactly what you are doing, however, when you and your partner both use work styles consistently while dealing with an issue. Although it may be hard to do this, we're convinced it's worth the effort. Think about the most recent experience you and your partner had in which the two of you were able to use work styles around a difficult issue. As you finished your discussion:

How did you feel about yourself, about how you related to your partner?

How did you feel about your partner?

How did you feel about the relationship you two share together?

SUMMING UP

Your self-concept and self-esteem include an accumulated set of pictures of yourself accompanied by self-evaluations and feelings about yourself. But fortunately that's not the whole story. Your self-concept and self-esteem are being maintained and/or altered *now* in your relationships with significant others, such as your partner or a friend. And whether your feeling down or whether you're feeling pleased about yourself you can *choose* to act in ways that say "I count" or in ways that say "I don't count." The same holds for your concept of partner and your esteem of partner, and for your concept of your relationship. When your decision is to count both yourself and your partner, the communication skills we've presented in this book can help you in carrying out that decision. If you don't like the esteem positions which you frequently assume and maintain, you can change them.

How you and your partner talk to each other offers a clue to the esteem you're building. Think for a moment of the situations today in which your messages and your partner's were either esteem-enchancing or esteem-diminishing.

Low-esteem messages limit growth, and these are more frequent in troubled relationships than in nurturing relationships. In nurturing relationships there are a lot of high-esteem messages exchanged; messages which support and encourage each other's growth.

Whose esteem are you building?

—Nobody's?

—Yours only?

—Your partner's only?

—Both yours and your partner's?

Remember, you don't have to sit around waiting for high esteem to "happen" to you and your partner. You can *choose* to count yourself and to count your partner, and you can *act* on your decision.

CHAPTER TWELVE

CONTRACTING TO WORK ON AN ISSUE

Let's look again at a couple working on a relationship issue. Remember this part of the dialogue from Chapter 9?

Debbie: "Some time ago we talked to each other about where our relationship was going. We decided that we'd live together for awhile. I've been doing some thinking about . . . and I don't want to just live together. I want to get married . . . I know I can anticipate how I'd feel living together. I'd have guilt. I wouldn't be able to handle it with my folks, especially since they live so close and I guess that's not really what I want at all anyhow. I'm willing to continue the relationship as it is but when we decide to make a committed relationship, I want it committed in marriage."

Eric: "I want us to live together before we marry . . . um, some day I do want to marry you but I also would like to live with you first . . . I guess partially it's because I've always wanted to do that, but I also would like to see how I adjust to a really close 24-hour-a-day contact with my mate, with you. I'd like to try it out before I do it just to see that I'm sure. I think I know a lot of how it would be already because we've spent an awful lot of time just staying at either one or the other's apartment. There's another thing too. I really enjoy being single, and I enjoy feeling free and you know about that. I also hear how you'd feel with your parents. Your parents would be kind of upset if we were to live together; but I mainly hear you want our relationship to be committed."

Debbie: "It is really scary for me to talk to you like this because when we first started seeing each other you told me about several girls you started dating, and when they started getting heavy, and you ran. But I guess I have to stand where I am and say that I do want marriage or no living together. I won't live with you, and I get mad at your fear of committing yourself. I get mad because I want to change you and I want to say to you, 'Hey, why don't you risk enough to get into it?' And sometimes I really get angry when I think you take such teeny steps towards risking any relationship. What do you hear me saying?"

THE MINI-CONTRACT

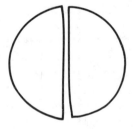

What's happening here is that Debbie and Eric have an *implicit* mini-contract to work on an issue. There are five parts that go into the mini-contract. You've already been introduced to all of the parts so we'll just mention them briefly here:

1. An issue is explicitly identified for discussion. It might be a topical issue, a personal issue of yours or your partner's, or it might be a relationship issue. If you need a little reminder about the kinds of issues included in each of these categories, you can refer back to Figure 6-1.

2. Both you and your partner have the intention to deal seriously with the issue at the present time.

3. You and your partner have an implicit consensus regarding your procedures for communicating. Again, if you want to

review the various procedural aspects of communication, refer back to the discussion of procedure-setting in Chapter 7.

4. You and your partner are both sharing complete and congruent awareness. You are both disclosing your Awareness Wheels, using the self-disclosure skills we introduced in Chapter 3 and have referred to throughout the book.

5. Both of you are communicating in ways which build self- *and* other esteem. That is, as we discussed in the last chapter, both of you are talking in ways which indicate "I count and I count you."

When you and your partner have an implicit mini-contract to work on an issue, as Debbie and Eric did, you won't explicitly identify an issue, declare your intentions to work, set procedures and so on. Rather, one of the partners will raise an issue and, by using a work style (Style III or IV) invite serious discussion, and the other will indicate acceptance of the invitation by responding in a work style. In short, you'll find yourselves using what we call *work-pattern* communication. We'll talk more about work patterns shortly. Here we simply want to note that a work pattern is a sequence of Style III and IV messages strung together. So when you and your partner have an implicit contract to work on an issue, you will be using work-pattern communication.

Mini-contracts are frequently implicit, but another way to create one is to do so *explicitly*. Remember the couple in Chapter 7? They created a mini-contract explicitly:

Amy: "You know we've been sitting with the checkbook, noticing the needs of the kids increasing financially—and now college is coming up. I guess the question on my mind is what are the possibilities of me going to work, and if I do, what are going to be the effects on both of us. I'd like to spend some time talking about this."

Don: "Well, I'd like to do that, too. I'd just as soon talk about it now. How about you?"

Amy: "Yeah, I would too. But I'm a bit concerned we may not have enough time."

Don: "Maybe we won't, but we can pick up on it again another night. I'd want to do that. All right?"

From this point on, Amy and Don begin working on Amy's personal issue about getting a job, and the other issues related to it—Don's feelings, impact on the family income, and so forth.

Amy and Don created their mini-contract quickly and efficiently. Let's look at the different parts of the mini-contract and see how they handled each:

1. Identifying an issue. In her first statement, Amy provided a brief context for the issue, then stated directly what the issues were—the possibility of her taking a job and the effects of this on herself, Don, and their relationship.

2. Intentions to work. Both Amy and Don indicate their intention to deal with the issue seriously by showing a willingness to talk about it in both their first and second statements.

3. Consensus regarding procedures. Don raises the procedural issue in this first statement when he indicates he would like to discuss Amy's concern right now and checks out his suggestion with her. Amy raises a specific procedural issue—timing—and Don follows up by agreeing that they may not have sufficient time to finish the issue. He also suggests that they don't necessarily have to complete their discussion, but can continue it at a later time, and again checks this out with Amy.

4. Sharing complete and congruent awareness. This is demonstrated directly when partners share their Awareness Wheels, as Don and Amy do in their discussion.

5. Building self-and other esteem. Don and Amy are demonstrating respect for both self and other by speaking for self and checking out.

Setting up a mini-contract isn't always as easy as it was for Amy and Don. Non-agreement about just one of the five major points, or even about one of the procedural points will disrupt effective communication about an issue. Have you ever had an important purchase or arrangement spoiled because you and the other person couldn't agree on one small point in the contract? Well, the same thing can happen with you and your partner. When one aspect of the mini-contract is out of sync, communication between you and your partner usually doesn't proceed effectively. When that happens, and it's not recognized, it's easy to begin thinking that your partner isn't interested, when in fact there's just a lack of a mini-contract.

Establishing a mini-contract says to your partner, "I'm willing and available to work with you on this issue in this way." We've found that when two people develop a mini-contract, demonstrating to one another real willingness to work on an issue openly, more than half of the difficulty is resolved. This is so because being able to achieve agreement to work reinforces each person's commitment to the relationship. When there is an actual or imagined question about one or both partners' commitment to the relationship, issues are difficult to resolve. When this commitment is no longer in doubt, resolving other issues becomes a simple matter.

We're amazed at how much partners can do to deal with issues and differences in a very short time, *when both people want to,* when the procedures for doing so are clearly spelled out, and when they communicate openly and supportively. We think you'll be amazed, too.

Deciding to work on an issue requires a mutual decision by you and your partner. Both of you must choose to do so, and it's an important choice for your relationship. The clearest demonstration of a mutual choice to work is when you and your partner are using work-pattern communication. Using a work pattern indicates that the various parts of the mini-contract are in effect. When you slip out of work-pattern communication, or can't get into it in the first place, you have a pretty good clue that one or more parts of the mini-contract are out of whack. At these times, it's useful to explicitly set up or renegotiate your mini-contract. So that you can better recognize when you and your partner are using work-pattern communication, we're going to describe it in some detail.

WORK-PATTERN COMMUNICATION

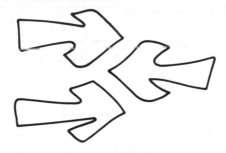

Let's begin by defining the work process. This process occurs when two partners (1) identify an issue, (2) have a mini-contract to work, and (3) deal with the issue by using a sequence of Style III and IV messages or Style IV alone. All three elements are necessary for a work process to occur. Just for fun, here's an example of Style III/IV sequences when there is no issue present. Two roommates are talking:

Mary: "I've been feeling very bored and restless this evening, and I think you are, too. I would like to do something to entertain myself, and hope you would like that, too. I'd like to discuss the idea of sharing a movie."

Jan: "I'm glad to know how you're feeling this evening. I feel the same way. It's a relief for me to know that you want to go to a movie, because that's what I'd like to do, too."

Mary: "I'm glad to hear that. I'd like to get the newspaper and find out what movies are playing. How does that sound to you?"

Sounds silly, doesn't it? Remember, when we discussed styles, we said each had its place. Everyday decisions like this are a natural for Style I:

> *Mary:* "How about a movie tonight?"
>
> *Jan:* "Sounds good. They're having a Charlie Chaplin festival at Har Mar."
>
> *Mary:* "Okay."

Not every issue that you and your partner have to deal with in your daily lives is an important one. And not every issue requires exploration and understanding. Sometimes work-pattern communication is inappropriate.

Developing a work process can be very useful at other times though. It's particularly useful when you want:

—To learn about yourself with your partner's help.

—To identify and heighten your awareness of some issues important to you.

—To deal with tension immediately when it occurs.

—To bring about changes in your relationship.

—To openly acknowledge something you like about yourself, your partner, or your relationship.

When you or your partner want any of these things, that's the time to move into work-pattern communication. Again, work-pattern communication happens when you and your partner string together a sequence of Style III and IV, or just Style IV messages. In developing a work pattern, the first three messages are of particular significance. The first Style III or IV message represents an *invitation* to your partner. It's a way of saying, "I want to work:"

> *Ann:* "Sometimes you say you agree with me, then later I learn you really didn't, and I think I've been shot down."

If your partner responds with a Style III or IV message, it represents an *acceptance* of your invitation, a way of saying, "Okay, I'm willing to work, too:"

Maggie: "Can you give me an example of what I do. It upsets me when you don't think I'm honest with you."

Finally, if the third statement in the sequence is also a Style III or IV message, you *confirm* your original intention to work, almost as if you're saying, "Good, I was serious about my invitation so I'll get on with it:"

Ann: "Well, I think your first reaction is to be agreeable without giving any thoughts to the merits, or to what you really think yourself. For example, two nights ago . . ."

In short, a work pattern develops when an invitation is made, accepted, and confirmed. All of this assumes, of course, that you and your partner have an issue you want to deal with. Sounds pretty easy, doesn't it? Well, it's actually harder than it sounds.

In a research project, 169 potential work patterns were identified in the communication of 31 average couples.[1] That is, these sequences began with either a Style III or Style IV statement. Among these potential work sequences, 69 percent ended after one message when the partner made a Style I or II statement, rejecting the invitation to work. Another 14 percent of the sequences ended after two statements; in these instances, the original invitation was accepted with a Style III or IV statement from the partner, but the invitation was not confirmed because the initial speaker made a Style I or II statement. So only about one out of every five potential work patterns actually became one.

Once the original invitation was confirmed, however, work-pattern communication was likely to continue. Among the sequences that actually became work, only 30 percent ended after three statements, 43 percent lasted from four to nine statements, and 27 percent continued for 10 statements or more. These data suggest that work begins in earnest only after the "confirm" message is sent, but once that's done, a work process is likely to go on for some time.

[1] In this research, couples were asked to spend five minutes discussing "the things that each of you does that irritates the other." Further data concerning the couple's behaviors and impact on their satisfaction with marriage is contained in, Daniel B. Wackman and Sherod Miller, "Analyzing Sequential Interaction Data: Two Empirical Studies," Paper presented at the International Communication Association Convention, Chicago, Ill., 1975.

Take-Aways and Non-Work Patterns.

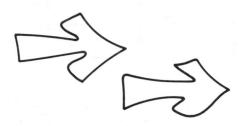

The key to developing a work pattern is to move past the third statement in the sequence. In our research, we have found that most couples can begin a potential work sequence. Only 3 of the 31 couples we tested communicated entirely in Styles I or II. On the other hand, only 7 of the couples communicated with a work pattern for as much as one-third of the 5-minute discussion. In other words, what frequently happens is that potential work sequences are stopped short after one or two statements. When this happens, one of the partners is using what we call a "take-away."

Consistent use of take-aways by one partner when the other persists in trying to start a work process results in an *impasse*. An impasse is a pattern in which there are frequent moves toward a work pattern, but which are consistently cut short by take-aways. Our research indicates impasse patterns cannot be maintained over a long period of time very readily; rather, partnerships who use them seem to move to one of two nonwork patterns after a while. (We'll have much more to say about several kinds of impasse patterns in the next chapter, since overcoming impasses is one of the keys to dealing with issues constructively.)

The Avoidance Pattern.

The first kind of nonwork pattern results from a consistent use of Style I take-aways. When a Style I take-away is used, partners usually move away from the issue. Recall the main intention in Style I—to keep things going smoothly. Often the easiest way to attempt to keep things on an even keel is to ignore or avoid issues by making irrelevant conversation or joking. We call the pattern that develops a *nonwork avoidance pattern*.

Lynn: "I've been experiencing a lot of tension at work and I'm concerned that I'm bringing it back home with me. I'm afraid that it might be causing tension for you, too, and I really don't want that to happen. I'd like to talk about this with you."

Bill: "I have noticed that you seem kind of edgy and dragged out lately. But I think things will probably ease up for you. Maybe if we do some things you enjoy you can relax."

Lynn: "I don't really think so. I'm getting a lot of pressure these days to complete this project, but I don't think it will be done for some time. So the tension is likely to increase, if anything."

Bill: (smiling) "I'll get you some tranquilizers so you can calm down."

Here Bill tries to joke with Lynn to relieve the tension, but the effect is more likely to be that Lynn will interpret his message as an attempt to avoid the issue—and perhaps as a put-down. Avoiding an issue by shifting the conversation to another topic or by joking about it would seem to be a pretty ineffective way to deal with it because usually the issue persists and resurfaces again. But many couples do lock themselves into an avoidance pattern, and fail to confront any issues directly.

The Conflict Pattern.

The second kind of nonwork pattern results when Style II take-aways are used consistently. Again, recall the main intentions of Style II—to change your partner and control the situation. Style II take-aways seem to express this intention pretty clearly, and when they occur, conflict often results. The partner using Style II take-aways seems to be trying to change the other person or put down the other's attempts to explore the issue and deal with it directly. Often arguments or fights ensue as Style II accusations, blames, and demands are traded back and forth. We call the resulting sequence of Style II statements a *nonwork conflict pattern.*

Lynn: "I've been experiencing a lot of tension at work and I'm concerned that I'm bringing it back home with me. I'm afraid that it might be causing tension for you, too, and I really don't want that to happen. I'd like to talk about this with you."

Bill: "Yeah. You've been tough to live with recently. You're putting a lot of pressure on me and the kids."

Lynn: "I'm getting a lot of pressure these days to complete this project, but I don't think it will be done for some time. So the tension is likely to increase, if anything."

Bill: "That doesn't give you any right to dump it on us at home!"

Lynn: "Well, you certainly aren't much help to me! You know how busy I've been, but you haven't lifted a hand to help me around here!"

Bill: "What do you mean? I cooked dinner the last two nights. Did you forget that already?"

Lynn: "But those were the first two times in over a month. Big deal!"

Bill responds to Lynn's work attempt by accusing her and telling her what she shouldn't be doing. These kinds of Style II statements are tough for most of us to handle, but when they are used, as in this example, when one partner is trying to work on a serious issue, they often lead to explosions. Bill and Lynn's trading of accusations and blame is a typical result of using Style II take-aways. It's obvious that this nonwork conflict pattern cannot deal with the issue effectively, yet many couples frequently use it when issues arise. Just as with the avoidance pattern, partners locked into the conflict pattern do not resolve their issues very often. But worse yet, the conflict pattern often results in such bad feelings between partners that the positives in their relationship are lost, and continuation of the relationship becomes *the* major issue.

Starting a Work Process.

Take-aways keep you and your partner from developing a work process. Remember the definition of a work process: an issue is identified, a mini-contract exists, and the issue is dealt with using a sequence of Style III and IV messages.

But a work process doesn't just start itself when an issue occurs. Rather, it involves a movement from nonwork Styles (I and II) to the work Styles (III and IV). So the question of how to start a work process becomes one of how to shift into Styles III and IV. Most often the shift occurs in the process of identifying the issue. As partners begin to focus on an issue, particularly a personal or relationship issue, they usually find themselves shifting from Style I to another style. That's because the feelings which are frequently involved in these kinds of issues are difficult to express using Style I.

Remember how we set up the figure showing the different styles in the shape of a diamond? We did this because it is difficult to move directly from Style I into Style IV where the most effective work occurs. When an issue arises, one or both partners often begin to send Style II messages, in which tension or feelings are expressed indirectly. Then, assuming the partners are effective communicators, they will become aware of what's happening and shift into Style IV, identifying the issue and talking about it directly and openly. When they reach a point where each has a clear understanding of "where they're coming from," the issue is likely to be settled with only an action statement or two from each. With the issue settled, they shift back to Style I and just enjoy themselves.

Sometimes the Style IV part of their interaction makes clear that they each want very different things. In this case, an additional problem-solving or conflict-negotiating phase is helpful. If the issue is topical, or perhaps personal, they may move into Style III, explore various alternative solutions at an intellectual level, then shift back to Style IV as they commit themselves with action statements. However, if the conflict involves a relationship issue, their problem-solving efforts will probably remain in a Style IV pattern until closure. Full disclosure, understanding, and commitments to act are the essentials for resolving relationship issues.

We have emphasized that the move from a general topical conversation to a personal or relationship issue often involves a corresponding shift from Style I to II as the feelings involved in the issue are expressed indirectly. And when both partners begin to use Style III or IV, a work process is started. But sometimes a work process is started by shifting from Style I to Style III to "safely test the waters." This happens most often when one partner raises an issue from the past, or what may become an issue in the future, with the intention of exploring or elaborating on it. Usually, strong feelings are absent at that moment although the issue may have been a highly emotional one in the past.

However it begins, a work process will only start when both partners shift to the work styles and begin stringing work statements together. The key point is that *both* partners have to make the shift. If only one of them does, an impasse will result, and when it does, steps to overcome the impasse will be necessary— either renegotiating your mini-contract, or possibly deciding not to work at that point in time.

Once partners have developed a work process, it is likely to continue for some time. Sometimes impasses crop up again, particularly when angry feelings arise. The impasses can usually be resolved by pausing briefly to look at which part of your mini-contract is out of sync, then moving back into the work process.

Both Styles III and IV are work styles, but you cannot deal effectively with a difficult issue if you only use Style III. Style III is extremely useful for exploring an issue, looking at its background, and elaborating on it in general. But Style III used alone involves relatively little self-disclosure so the feelings behind issues are not disclosed. Further, Style III action statements typically express little commitment. So when a work process stays at Style III, it probably won't be effective for dealing completely and congruently with the issue. To focus directly and fully on an issue, particularly on both partners' present feelings and intentions regarding the issue, substantial doses of Style IV communication should be administered by both partners.

In closing this chapter, we'd like to restate something we strongly believe. The decision to work on an issue involves a voluntary choice. We believe it's anyone's right to choose *not to work*. Much of our emphasis in this chapter—and, in fact, throughout the book—has been on the usefulness of the work process for dealing directly with relationship issues. But we know there are times when partners really don't want to work on an issue. The reasons for this are too numerous to elaborate, but some common ones are that there isn't enough time, other people are present, one partner's feelings are too strong, and so forth.

Whatever the reasons, we think it's fine not to work, but we hope you'll disclose this directly to your partner.

> *Jeff:* "There's been something happening at work that bothers me a lot. I'd like to talk it through with you to try to understand it better. Are you up to that now?"
>
> *Jill:* "Not really, Jeff. I have to do some errands and some shopping before the stores close. I want to try to help you though. How about if we talk when I get back? I should be home by 9:30."

It can be pretty frustrating for both you and your partner when one of you wants to get work started and the other doesn't, but you don't say so. That's when heavy conflicts and bad feelings build. So feel free to work or not to work, but be direct with your partner about your intention.

CHAPTER THIRTEEN

TROUBLE SHOOTING: WHAT CAN GO WRONG AND HOW TO DEAL WITH IT

As we have seen, there are many different pieces and dimensions in communication. By this time, you may be holding your head and saying, "But it's all so complicated!" We agree. Don't expect to be an effective communicator immediately. It takes a lot of practice and clear intentions. These are points to keep in mind when you're working on your relationship:

1. Tune into your sensations, interpretations, feelings, intentions, and actions.

2. Use the self-disclosure skills to express your self-awareness.

3. Check out your partner's self-awareness.

4. Use the shared meaning process to increase accuracy.

5. Set up a mini-contract when you want to work on an issue.

6. Establish and maintain mutual I count/I count you attitudes.

Perhaps a list of half a dozen items makes the whole process seem a little less awesome. If it does, we're glad. But communicating effectively remains a complicated, intricate process where dozens of things can go wrong. When something does go wrong, though, you don't have to remain helpless; there are a number of ways to deal with it. That's what this chapter is about: trouble shooting when difficulties crop up.

IMPASSES: THE MAJOR BARRIER TO WORKING ON YOUR RELATIONSHIP

As we discussed in the last chapter, effective work on your relationship occurs when you and your partner have a mini-contract. And the best index of a mini-contract is work pattern communication. Similarly, the best index of when a mini-contract is missing is when you and your partner are not using a work pattern, particularly when you are stuck in an impasse pattern. Let's look a bit more closely at impasses.

Actually, there are two distinct types of impasses. We call the first type a *persistence* impasse. What happens here is that partner A persists toward work by making Style III or IV statements. At the same time, partner B resists work by making Style I or II statements. A persistence impasse is diagrammed in Figure 13-1.

Work (III or IV)   A   A   A   A   A   A

Nonwork (I or II)   B   B   B   B   B   B

Figure 13-1. Persistence Impasse Pattern.

An *ambivalence* impasse is the second type. Here partner A invites work with a Style III or IV statement, and partner B accepts the invitation by responding with a Style III or IV statement. But partner A does not confirm the invitation; rather s/he returns a Style I or II statement, moving away from work. An ambivalence impasse is shown in Figure 13-2:

Work (III or IV)   AB   AB   AB

Nonwork (I or II)   AB   AB   AB

Figure 13-2. Ambivalence Impasse Pattern.

The patterns we have shown in the figures are simplifications of what really happens, of course, since partners rarely communicate totally with an impasse pattern. What happens more typically is that impasses are interspersed with nonwork (a sequence of Style I or II statements). An example of this is shown in Figure 13-3, where persistence impasse alternates with nonwork.

Work (III or IV)   A   A   A   A   A

Nonwork (I or II)   B   BABAB   BAB   B   BAB

Nonwork (I or II)

Figure 13-3. Alternating Pattern of
Persistence Impasse and Nonwork.

The patterns we presented have all shown partner A initiating work and partner B either rejecting work (persistence impasse) or accepting the work invitation but having A disconfirm the original invitation (ambivalence impasse). It is possible for the initiation to shift between partners, for example, with A persisting toward work for a while, then later B persisting toward work without A accepting the work invitation. But our research indicates this doesn't happen very often. Rather, more typically, only one partner initiates work, as we have shown in the figures. Further, few couples shift between the two kinds of impasses; most couples get stuck in only one type of impasse.

You can recognize when you and your partner are missing a mini-contract by looking for impasses. If things don't seem to be going right, such as anger is building up, you find yourself confused about the issue, and so forth, step back and look at your communication. See if one of the impasse patterns has cropped up. The impasse may be preventing you from getting work started, or it may develop in the middle of work. But in either case, Style I or II statements by you or your partner will provide a clear behavioral indication that the two of you don't have a mini-contract at that time. At this point, you can trouble shoot by looking at your mini-contract.

LOOKING AT YOUR MINI-CONTRACT

We suggest that you and your partner step back and look at your interaction when you think things aren't going well. If you find

yourself in an impasse, it's time to examine your mini-contract, if you have one, and maybe negotiate a new one.

Checking Out Intentions.

Perhaps the first part of the mini-contract to examine is intentions—your own and your partner's. Look first at your intentions regarding work. Remember, if both of you don't have an intention to work, it's not going to happen. When you look for your hidden intentions, you're trying to discover the hidden agenda that both you and your partner may bring to the interaction. For example, one of you may simply want to hassle the other, or both of you may want to get your own way. Ask yourself, "Do I really want to work now?"

> *Bill:* "I feel unhappy about your trip this weekend."
>
> *Lois:* "Oh? I'm glad you're sharing that with me. I'm excited about going. What's making you unhappy?"
>
> *Bill:* "How can you be happy about it when I tell you how I feel?"

In this example Bill's real intention is to change his partner's feelings, not to work. Intentions to work are slippery because communication so easily slips into Style II (manipulating, blaming and labeling) or into a mixed Style III/II (searching with little intention of finding).

Sometimes it's tough to identify whether or not you have an intention to work. It may be that one of you is trying to subtly force work when the other doesn't want to. Or sometimes a partner will agree tó work when s/he is not ready to do so.

> Sue: "I'd like to talk about something in our love-making that bothers me. Are you willing to do that now?"
>
> Paul: (lowering his magazine and putting it in his lap) "Sure."
>
> Sue: "Well, it's just that, sometimes I don't think it's a very affectionate kind of thing. I miss sometimes holding and caressing."
>
> Paul: (flipping through magazine) "Well, I can see that."
>
> Sue: "When you keep looking at your magazine, and when your answers are so brief, I get the idea that you're not really interested in talking about this right now even though you said you were. Is that true? I'd rather that you tell me so."

When it becomes apparent to either partner that one may not want to work, it's best to stop talking about the original issue and zero in on intentions directly, as illustrated by Sue's comment to Paul.

Finding these intentions can be difficult because they are elusive. But as elusive and slippery as they may be, consciously focusing on your intentions can reveal your attitudes toward work at that moment, and you can discover if your intentions are causing difficulties in trying to work on your relationship.

All of us do some funny things with our intentions at times. For example, you may withhold your intentions from your partner by failing to reveal mixed intentions when you have them. Or you may fail to let your partner know what you hope the outcome of your discussion will be when you have a particular direction in mind. But focusing on your intentions directly can clarify them and move you back into work. Remember, though, you and your partner have the right not to work. No one feels like working all the time or every time your partner wants to. The hassles start when you don't directly express your intention not to work.

New conflicts are a second aspect of intentions to look for. Life being what it is, it's not unusual for you and your partner to have conflicting intentions. There is a way to deal with this kind of trouble. Shift your focus from what each of you *want to do* to what each of you *want for yourself.*

> *Martha:* "I want to stay home tonight, and you want to go out. Let's see what it will do for us if we reverse positions and each talk about what we'd get out of it if we stayed home or if we went out. Okay?"
>
> *Don:* "Okay. What I want is to do some socializing with other people."
>
> *Martha:* "I wouldn't mind that. When I said I wanted to stay home, what I had in mind was I want to avoid getting back in the car and on the highway. I've been driving around all day, and I can't stand the thought of any more traffic today."
>
> *Don:* "How would it be then if we invite somebody over here?"
>
> *Martha:* "At this hour? What would we tell them?"
>
> *Don:* "We'll tell it like it is. We didn't want to go out, but we wanted to see them and would they mind driving over in return for some pizza and good company. How's that for an offer?"

When you talk with your partner about what each of you wants for yourself at that moment it's likely to provide a more expanded and elaborated range of choices, and therefore the two of you may arrive at a more mutually satisfying decision. Using the same process, Don and Martha might have arrived at any one of a number of alternative solutions to their individual wants—Don went out and Martha stayed home; or, they went out together to a corner tap instead of driving across town.

Clarifying the Issue.

If both of you discover that you want to work, it's time to look at other parts of the mini-contract. Next you might want to move to the issue. Often work doesn't get started because an issue has not been clearly identified. We have talked about how easy it is to confuse issues, for example, by focusing on a topic issue when a relationship issue is more significant at the time. Let's look at an example.

Andy: "I'm feeling disappointed that you don't understand how I'm feeling." (IV/II mixed style)

Joan: "You sound really ticked off. If you are, I wish you'd say so and not try to be reasonable."

Andy: "Well, I am ticked! As much at myself as at you. I'm trying to be open about having my sister visit, but I'm just getting angrier the longer we go on."

Joan: "What's the anger about? I don't think you feel so accepting about her visit."

Andy: "You know, I think you're right. I really don't want her to come for that long, and I guess that's coming through. I get awfully uncomfortable when we're together for more than a couple of days."

Here Joan shifts the focus directly to Andy's feelings and thinking. In the process, they clarify what the major issue is in their discussion—Andy's personal issue concerning his response to his sister.

Sometimes issues become confused because a number of different ones are involved in a discussion. When this happens, it often helps to list the various issues (perhaps even writing them down) and take them one at a time. The purpose of this procedure is simply to help clarify the issue: to keep work from getting bogged down in confusion over what is being discussed.

Setting Procedures.

Even when both of you want to work and you have clarified your issue, an impasse may develop because you lack consensus about procedures. Perhaps you think there isn't enough time so you begin rushing to get all your feelings out and inadvertently shift to Style II. Or other people may be present so you begin to withhold information, or talk indirectly, using Style I. When you find yourselves in an impasse, it often helps to quickly sort through the various procedural factors:

—whose issue

—who is included

—where to talk

—when to talk

—how to talk

—how much energy you have

—how long to talk

—how to stop talking

Disagreement about any of these factors can interfere with work, resulting in an impasse as one partner shifts to a nonwork style. Clarifying the procedural issue can get you back on the track, or help you to set another time for working on the issue.

Sharing Complete and Congruent Awareness.

The first three parts of the mini-contract—intentions, issue, and procedure—can be set early in a work process. The next two parts—sharing awareness and building esteem—generally emerge during the process since they involve the use of particular communication skills. However, failure to use these skills can cause an impasse which prevents you and your partner from beginning a work process, as well as creating an impasse during a work process.

You can use the Awareness Wheel to see whether incomplete or incongruent self-awareness is causing an impasse. Ask yourself what's in your own wheel, and look at how you are expressing your self-awareness.

> Jim: "Hey, we're beginning to sound like a couple of Style II heavyweights. And I thought we would be able to handle this issue openly. What gave me a jolt just now was suddenly realizing I was about to try and get even with you."

> Kay: "You're right. We left off working quite a ways back. Thinking back, I started to get sore when you brought up something that happened weeks ago—but I didn't tell you I was sore about that. I remember now, I accused you of fault-finding."

> *Jim:* "And I got sore when you did that, but I didn't tell you. Instead, I think I started laying a trap for you with some leading questions. Man, it's sure easy to slip back into old patterns!"
>
> *Kay:* "I feel ready to get back to the issue now. How about you?"

Or when disclosing your awareness, focus on whether or not you're using some of the basic skills, such as speaking for self.

> *Pete:* "You ought to try it, at least."
>
> *Jean:* "I get my back up when I hear 'ought.' I start feeling pushed and don't even want to consider it."
>
> *Pete:* "Okay, I read you. Let me play that again: I wish you'd try it. I really think you'd find it worthwhile. And if you didn't, I'd find it easier to accept than if you had never really tested it out."

Neglecting to use the self-disclosure skills or the awareness-of-other skills often results in shifting to Styles I or II. Sometimes this occurs because of incomplete self-awareness, and at other times because you forget to use the skills; but in either case, an impasse results. When you are able to step back and identify your own incomplete or incongruent awareness, often it will feel like finding a missing piece in a jigsaw puzzle. Or when you and your partner step back and identify how you're expressing—or failing to express—your self-awareness, you'll begin to see some of the things each of you is doing which may be keeping you from dealing with the issue. Then you'll be able to change your communication, overcome the impasse, and begin to work on the issue.

Building Esteem.

Finally, when you examine your mini-contract, look at your attitudes toward yourself and your partner. Are you really counting both self and partner?

> *Randy:* "I'm feeling lousy today. I'm not sure what it's about, but I don't want to be bothered."
>
> *Liz:* "What do you mean you don't want to be bothered? That sounds as though I'm a bother to you most of the time."

Randy: "No! No, I don't mean that at all. I think we're almost getting into something that I don't want to get into right now. Are you willing to do a shared meaning with my message to you?"

Liz: "Okay."

Randy: "What I'm trying to say is that I'm in a down mood, generally irritable. I don't want to be confronted with making any decisions till I'm out of it. Right now, when we're together, I'd like to just chitchat, talk about the Vikings, and stuff."

Liz: "I hear you saying you're in a low and edgy mood and don't want to talk about anything heavier than the Vikings vs. the Packers. I'm also thinking that you don't want to deal with the issue of our trip, since that's what I started to bring up just when you said you felt lousy."

Randy: "Yeah, that's it. The trip or anything else heavy. I'd be willing to get back to that tonight, but right now, I'd just like to relax and not have to think much. Okay with you?"

Liz: "Sure. Tonight's soon enough. The Packers don't stand a chance . . . "

In this example, Randy did a good job of counting himself initially, but ended up with a statement that sounded like a put-down of Liz. Naturally, that was the part of his message that had the most impact on Liz. When Randy realized what had happened, he asked for a shared meaning so he could be better understood.

Put-downs of your partner are particularly likely to create impasses since they so frequently are followed by Style II responses. But as we saw in the example, interaction does not have to move to conflict when a put-down occurs. However, stepping back and talking about it, perhaps using a shared meaning, is often necessary.

TROUBLES THAT GO BEYOND COMMUNICATION

Up to this point, we've focused on identifying impasses as clues to communication difficulties and using the mini-contract to overcome them. At this point, we want to shift gears and focus on difficulties that go beyond straight communication skills.

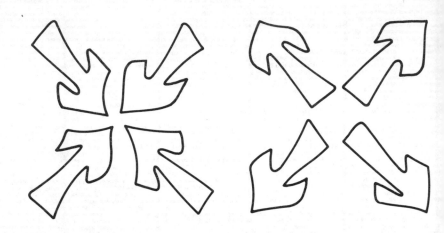

Too Much Communication.

"All work . . ."

One big trouble that you and your partner can get into is to come to believe that you should be working on your relationship all of the time. Throughout these pages, we've tried to let you know that we don't believe relationships are all work. Quite the contrary, we believe work is essential for maintaining and developing your relationship, but we also believe the need for work is *only occasional.* When you and your partner don't know how to work, you're more vulnerable as a partnership, and less likely to maximize your potentials together and apart. But relationships are for living—playing, savoring, experiencing, and enjoying. And since work involves some personal and interpersonal tensions, to live in a continual state of work would be just plain crazy!

Some partners think they have to be "working" all the time to be okay. They're hooked on work. Part of their self-esteem comes from the feeling of being continually "at work." In a strange sort of way, work becomes their "fun." This pattern is one you and your partner could slip into if all you see are problems in your relationship, or if you have a hard time playing at anything. It's an easy pattern to slip into, too, if you think that playing is only a way of avoiding "the never-ending series of real-life issues." That, we believe, is not what relationships are about!

"All We Do Is Talk!"

This issue often arises when partners discuss issues in their relationship interminably but don't arrive at solutions. Earlier in the book, we talked about avoiding both preclosure on issues and failure to achieve closure. When partners succeed in avoiding preclosure but then don't develop any solutions, the complaint that "all we do is talk" is likely to surface. One way to deal with this problem is for each partner to pay attention to the action component of his/her Awareness Wheel and make commitments for action. Most solutions are not written in stone for all ages. Usually they can be modified if they turn out to be unsatisfactory. So it's important to make commitments to action, monitor the solutions by maintaining self-awareness, and change actions at a later point if necessary.

Failure to reach solutions isn't the only reason this issue crops up. Sometimes partners are very effective in developing solutions, but have great difficulty in putting them into action. Usually what happens is that the solutions are basically statements of goals, and when these goals don't just happen, the complaint that "all we do is talk" arises. Here again, partners should pay more attention to the action dimension of their wheels, perhaps develop an "action plan" to turn their agreed-upon goals into specific actions to which they commit themselves.

Both of these "communication" issues do relate to the ways in which partners communicate together. And changing the communication skills each partner uses can go a long way toward resolving them. But sometimes the issues involve other relationship issues, such as a clash of goals or values, different levels of commitment to the relationship, and so forth. To the extent that these kinds of concerns are involved, more than changes in communication may be necessary.

Esteem Issues.

"I Count Only If You Say So."

Waiting to validate your own self-esteem through approval by your partner is another source of trouble for relationships. You can choose to count and value yourself, and your partner as well, regardless of how your partner treats you. Further, you have a responsibility to count yourself. How can you expect your partner or anyone else to value you, if you don't value yourself? And when you do count yourself without blaming, attacking, or making demands on your partner, your partner probably will come to view you in the same way that you view yourself.

But what if you *really* don't feel worthwhile? What if you don't think you count? We think you can *choose* to count yourself in your relationship with others even when you feel down, worthless, etc. You can do this by treating your no-count feelings as an important part of your experience. Work on getting in touch with these feelings when they occur, see what they're all about, and deal with them by yourself, or perhaps with your partner's help. (Sometimes it may even be useful to consult a counselor or therapist to help you get completely and congruently in touch with your awareness.) But however you do it, the important point is that you can count yourself by treating your negative feelings about yourself as significant.

"You Count Only If I Say So."

This is another way of saying, "you'd be nothing without me," and is a source of trouble for your relationship. When you relate to your partner in this way, you're over-estimating your own importance and, we think, fooling yourself. You are missing and deprecating your partner's unique assets when you treat him/her in this way. If you find yourself taking responsibility for your partner's self-esteem, we invite you to consider these questions: What do you get out of trying to be in charge of your partner? What do you lose by doing this? We think you'll find that your losses far out-number your gains.

"I Think You Count So You Must, Too."

We all have a touch of Florence Nightingale in us. But if your partner doesn't count him/herself,, you can't really do the counting for him/her. You can *contribute* to your partner's self-esteem by communicating that s/he counts to you, but in the end, everyone is in charge of their *own* esteem.

In all of the "no-count" situations we've just described, only consistent counting of yourself and your partner *without* getting hooked by imagined impotence can sustain your relationship.

Basic Relationship Issues.

"But We Can't Talk About That."

Sometimes, one or both partners decide that certain topics are taboo. Often this occurs when you or your partner won't tell the other what it is you see and what meaning you make out of what you're seeing. When this happens, reality is denied, distorted, or disconfirmed, instead of being dealt with directly. If some issues or topics are taboo, fear controls the relationship and limits growth. Inability to discuss certain issues is often symptomatic of more significant issues in the relationship related to honesty, trust, and commitment.

"What If You Really Knew Me?"

When you deliberately report distorted and/or incomplete self-awareness, you're cheating yourself. Unless both of you are committed to honesty, we believe that neither you nor your relationship will grow. We don't think people are dishonest because they're bad; rather, we believe that they fear real or imagined consequences. One common fear in partnerships is related to the notion that if you really let your partner know who you are or what you want, s/he will reject you, and possibly even leave. But that is an inherent risk in all growth. If you don't take the risk, you are limiting your own and your partner's initiative to stay, to leave, to grow.

Honesty doesn't arrive in one big "moment of truth." Honesty is a minute-by-minute, on-going process. The process involves maintaining awareness of yourself, your partner, and your relationship, and it also involves *sharing* this awareness with your partner.

"We're Incompatible."

Partners sometimes discover conflicts between important values, goals, and wants. When this is discovered early, it can lead to termination of the relationship. But as partners grow and change, sometimes serious discrepancies in values, goals, and wants arise after years of a relationship. Here a lot depends on what you want—to work through the discrepancies to enhance the quality and meaning of your relationship, to terminate the relationship, or to settle for some chronic and possibly unsatisfactory "stand off."

"Can I Believe You?"

Sometimes conflict will arise when your partner expresses an intention, but your interpretation of his/her behavior doesn't match the expressed intention. As a general rule, assuming that both of you are committed to being honest with each other, you will reveal your doubts and describe what you saw or heard which led to your interpretation. This feedback may enable your partner to either get in better touch with his own intentions and correct his verbal messages to you, or understand how you are viewing his behavior and go on to reveal more information to clarify the contradiction. However, if over the long haul, you doubt that your partner's being honest with you, that's something to deal with directly. The issue shifts from who is interpreting or revealing accurately to discussing and questioning basic issues of honesty and trust. And in the extreme, the issue becomes whether or not to continue the relationship.

NEVER DEALING WITH ISSUES EFFECTIVELY

Constant failure to deal effectively with an issue in your relationship frequently means you and your partner have a serious problem. Some of the reasons for this and ways in which this problem is expressed were discussed in the last section. This is a serious problem because it raises the very issue of the continuation of your relationship. You do have alternatives, however.

One alternative is to accept the relationship as it is, and adjust to it. To a large extent, this may mean letting your partner determine your personal growth.

A second alternative is to blast your partner, blame him/her for the pattern of your relationship, and try to force him/her to change. If you choose this alternative, it means that you are trying to take charge of your partner and determine his/her growth.

A third alternative for you is captured by the phrase: "be true to yourself." Choosing this alternative means you focus on your own growth and development and try to work to help your partner and your relationship grow. This may be a difficult option to use consistently but you do have major strengths for maintaining it: (1) your own awareness, particularly awareness of your short-term and long-term intentions for yourself and your relationship; (2) your skills for disclosing self-awareness and helping your partner to do the same.

We think there are several points to keep in mind if you choose the third alternative. Change usually is slow, and it often involves pain for yourself, your partner, and your relationship.

You can ask for change from your partner. This is a lot different from demanding change. If you lose the focus on yourself and your contribution to the relationship, it's easy to slip into demanding change. And the formula, "If you change, I'll change," usually results in no change. But don't forget: since your partnership is an interdependent system, if you change one part of it—yourself— other parts and the relationship will also change. These changes may not be the ones you'd like, but they will occur.

It is your life, so after trying to work with your partner on your relationship and failing, you may want to choose the option of leaving. But an important part of your life is your interdependence with others, and a major part of what you want for yourself in the long-run is likely to involve what you want from your relationships with others, particularly your intimate partner.

MISUSE OF YOUR AWARENESS AND SKILLS

We've been focusing on trouble shooting when communication is not going well or when there are deeper issues in your relationship. In this closing section, we are going to shift and look at misuse of awareness and skills.

Self-awareness and communication skills are powerful forces for helping relationships to develop, but they can be misused. Two common ways in which they are misused are trying to force change in your partner, and trying to force others to be open with you. These things typically happen for one of two reasons. First, misuse occurs when you have the Style II intentions to control and force change. Second, it occurs when you lose sight of the fact that you have long-term intentions, as well as short-term ones. We've talked at length about the first reason; so, here we'll focus on the second.

Awareness and skills are powerful, but they can also be seductive. So be aware how you use them in non-intimate relationships, particularly when the other person is less aware and less skilled. Remember that one of the most important intentions you have is what you want from your relationship, not just what you want your own behavior to be. For example, it's not just "I want to be more open with you," but also—and perhaps more importantly—"I want to have a congruent relationship with you." This may mean not being completely open with another person in the present for any number of reasons—lack of history with another person, the other person isn't ready to return your openness, the other person may not have the skills to be open with you, the situation is inappropriate, etc.

Furthermore, keep in mind that close, intimate, open relationships are not the only legitimate and satisfying kind. Closeness and intimacy require time and energy, but you may not want this in certain relationships. Yet you can still gain many rewards from them.

In short, when you are in non-intimate relationships, take the other person's rights into account as you make use of your awareness and skills. If you really do care about the other person, there is no better way to show you care than to explicitly negotiate a mini-contract with him/her before trying to be open. The same consideration also applies, of course, if your intimate partner lacks awareness and skills. In fact, the misuse of awareness and skills is the major reason we suggest that you read ALIVE AND AWARE with your partner. Better yet, we think it's a good idea to join a Couple Communication group with your partner to make your learning of new awareness and skills together easier and more effective.

KEY IDEAS FROM SECTION IV

1. Self/other esteem building messages are essential to personal and relationship development.

2. Dealing with an issue effectively requires a mini-contract to work on the issue.

3. A mini-contract has five parts:
   —Identification of an issue
   —Intention of both partners to work
   —Procedural consensus
   —Complete and congruent self disclosure by both partners
   —Both partners use an I count/I count you orientation

4. Work pattern communication is an index to a mini-contract.

5. When impasses develop, a mini-contract is missing. Trouble shoot by looking at the different parts of your mini-contract.

CHAPTER FOURTEEN

POSTSCRIPT: COMMUNICATION AND RELATIONSHIPS

It may seem odd that we have spent a whole book talking about communication skills for partners. After all, people have been talking to each other for thousands of years. But the fact is, our forms of communication have developed over centuries of time in which people communicated from a stance of authority and submission rather than equality, distance rather than intimacy, and disguise rather than openness. These forms of communication, developed in the past, simply are not compatible with the objectives of today's partners. In this day and time, people are seeking relationships characterized by equality, intimacy, and openness.

In this book, we have viewed communication as both a *vehicle* for creating relationships and as an *index* of relationships. In both instances, however, communication is not an end in itself. As a vehicle for creating relationships, it can be an effective means of exchanging important information. As an index of relationship, it provides ways of understanding significant aspects of the nature of a relationship, for example, by monitoring time spent in verbal communication, degree of self-disclosure, styles of communication, the focus of conversations, types of issues being handled, and so forth.

While we have presented skills to help you create equality, intimacy, and openness in your relationships, communication itself is not a panacea—a "cure all." Communication is a means for expressing and demonstrating the unique life and energy of each person in a relationship and the process of the partnership. It supports and reflects both the life within each of us and between the two of us.

But communication is more than this too. It can help you and your partner effectively deal with change. Throughout ALIVE AND AWARE, we have assumed that people and relationships are constantly changing. We believe this is true because there are so many sources for change in our present society. Many of these sources are external ones: education, job changes, input from television and other media, friends, children, relatives, etc. A number of internal sources also exist, such as physical maturation, new experiences and ideas, feelings, emerging values, wants, and dreams, both your own and your partner's. Because so many sources for change exist, each person is constantly confronted with choices for self and for the relationship.

To deal with and even help create change, we've presented a set of frameworks for helping you increase awareness of yourself, your partner, and the process of your relationship, and communication skills and principles for putting this awareness into action. The basic outcome we think you'll experience, as you use the frameworks, skills, and principles, will be a feeling of greater control over your life and increased self-reliance, self-direction, and self-respect. Further, we think experimentation with your increased awareness and new skills will help you and your partner discover new alternatives in your relationship—and yield greater flexibility and variety in your lives.

Perhaps what we have been saying can be condensed to three broad principles for helping yourself, your partner, and your relationship to grow.

1. Maintain self-awareness and disclose it to your partner.

2. Check out and help your partner disclose his/her own self-awareness.

3. Build self/other esteem by dealing directly with issues in your relationship.

When you and your partner follow these three principles, you'll find yourselves making more explicit choices for your relationship. Then you will be able to arrange the relationship "arrows" as you choose:

OUR ASSUMPTIONS

In ALIVE AND AWARE we have made a series of assumptions about people and relationships. Many of these assumptions have already been stated; others have not. Here, we are simply going to list them to let you see how they fit with your own views.

1. I am the authority on my own experience.

2. My contribution to our relationship is under my control; my partner's contribution is not.

3. My partner's behavior does not cause mine; I always have choices for how I respond.

4. I cannot really count myself unless I count my partner too.

5. I cannot force my partner to either count or discount him/herself; my partner cannot force me to count or discount myself, either.

6. My behavior—being alive and aware—makes me attractive.

7. Awareness is a two-edged sword (it can be a blessing or a curse); once I'm aware, I cannot *not* be aware.

8. How I deal with my awareness is my choice.

9. Working toward complete and congruent self-awareness is a life style.

10. Awareness expands my choices; my choices expand my awareness.

11. When I change, my relationship changes.

12. Waiting for my partner to change so I can change equals no change.

13. I can ask my partner to change.

14. Disagreements and conflicts between myself and my partner are inevitable; they provide opportunities for growth.

15. Relationship growth involves personal growth.

16. Growth and change come in phases.

17. Fear and pain are part of change; change disrupts the *status quo* and increases uncertainty.

18. Flexible partnerships accept uncertainty more easily and deal with it more constructively.

19. My partner and I can create our own solutions and develop our relationship, if we want to.

20. Supporting development for both myself and my partner increases our chances of gaining satisfaction from our relationship.

21. Effective communication takes time and energy.

22. Effective communicators are flexible communicators.

23. Work and play are both important in relationships.

24. The nature of our relationship is up to me and my partner—both of us.

We think these assumptions provide an accurate picture of the orientation that various people, who have developed highly satisfying relationships, hold regarding themselves and their relationships. As you read over our list, perhaps some additional assumptions came to mind. Nevertheless, we think that unless you acknowledge your own key contribution to your relationship and are committed to channeling energy into your partnership, you and your partner will have a difficult time developing a highly satisfying relationship.

If you do accept these basic assumptions and begin to spend time and energy building your relationships through both work and play, we think the communication frameworks, skills, and principles will help you develop them as you choose. And we hope you will find, as many other people have, that your efforts are rewarded with increases in the satisfactions you experience in your relationships.

APPENDIX
WHAT IS COUPLE COMMUNICATION?

Couple Communication is an educational program designed to improve communication between partners (married, friends, colleagues, living together, etc.) by focusing on the processes of flexible and effective communication. The program is not aimed at solving specific relationship problems. Rather, it's centered on teaching skills for dealing more effectively with developmental issues in relationships.

Couple Communication groups consist of five to seven partners meeting for three hours, one night per week for four consecutive weeks, with a Certified Instructor. Each session builds on the previous sessions.

The Program is structured and has specific goals. It emphasizes experiential learning, through exercises and feedback, supplemented by readings, short lectures and small group discussions to help couples better understand effective communication patterns. Partners identify specific communication skills they want to learn. Exercises enable them to practice these skills during group sessions. Partners experiment with the new communication skills between group sessions and report back to the group on their experience. ALIVE AND AWARE: IMPROVING COMMUNICATION IN RELATIONSHIPS discusses the frameworks and skills taught in the program. Both partners participate in a group, both learn frameworks and skills so they are better able to communicate with each other.

Before entering a group, both partners meet briefly with a Certified Instructor to learn more about the program (activities, time and place, etc.) and to decide if they want to enroll. Certified Instructors are generally people from a variety of professional backgrounds with considerable experience in relationship education. They have participated in our Instructor Training Program and have demonstrated their competence conducting Couple Communication groups.

If you would like the name of a Certified Instructor to contact near you, write us: Couple Communication, The Carriage House, 300 Clifton Ave., Minneapolis, Minnesota 55403.

INDEX

acknowledging sender's message
121-122
actions 48-49
leaving out 85
action statements 70-71
affective/cognitive 209
agreement/disagreement 155-160, 167
ambivalence impasse 261
avoidance pattern 254-255
Awareness Wheel 30-49, 130-134
how to use 49-51
why to use 51-52

behaviors, in Style I 175-178
in Style II 181-185
in Style III 190-192
in Style IV 202-204
in all styles, 208-209

checking out 105-109
closed questions 106
combined esteem positions 236-243
I count/I count you 242-243
I count/I don't count you 238-239
I don't count/I count you 240-241
I don't count/I don't count you
237-238
communication styles 172-211
Style I 173-180
Style II 180-189

Style III 189-195
Style IV 197-207
complete and congruent awareness
96-98, 267-268
confirming/clarifying 123-124
conflict pattern 255-256
consensus 163, 168

diselosure/receptivity 207-209
documenting 58-61

esteem 223-245, 268-269
issues 271-272
skills for building 243-244

feelings 39-43
leaving out 83
feeling statements 64-67
focus of communication 134-142
topic 135
self 135, 203
partner 136
relationship 136
mixed 137

impasses 254, 261-262
ambivalence impasse 261
persistance impasse 261-262

incongruent awareness 94-96
intentions 43-47, 263-265
  hidden 69, 109
  leaving out 84
  in Style I 173-174
  in Style II 180-181
  in Style III 189
  in Style IV 198-202
  in all styles 207-209
intention statements 67-69
interpretations 32-35
  leaving out 86-88
interpretive statements 62-64
issues 142-147
  relationship among 145-147
  types of 144

limited self-awareness 79-94
  problem of 88-93
  risks of 97

meta-talk 163
mini-contract 247-251, 262-269
misunderstanding, sources of 150-154
misuse of awareness and skills 275
mixed messages 212-218
  identifying 215-216
  coping with 216-218

nonwork patterns 254-256
  avoidance pattern 254-255
  conflict pattern 255-256

other esteem positions 232-236
  I count you 232-234
  I don't count you 234-236

persistence impasse 261-262
procedure-setting 165-167, 266-267

relationship issues 144, 273-274
relationships patterns 12-21, 281
  and time 19

around issues 17
  over time 18
  viable and limiting 20-21
relationship rules 160-164
relationship states 13-16
  apartness 15
  leading/supporting 14
  pushing/resisting 14
  togetherness 13

self esteem positions 227-231
  I count myself 227-229
  I don't count myself 229-231
sensations 35-39
  leaving out 82
sense statements 57-61
shared meaning process 110-128
  receiver-initiated 110, 113, 115, 122
  sender-initiated 111, 113, 116, 117, 119
  skills used 118-124
  uses of 124-126, 154
  when it won't work 126-127
skills for increasing awareness of other 105-109, 119-124, 203
skills for self disclosure 53-72, 76, 203
  risks in using 72-76
  speaking for self 54-57
  stating intention and asking for acknowledgment 119-120

take-aways 127, 254-255
  Style I 254
  Style II 255
troubles beyond communication 269-274

understanding/misunderstanding 148-155

why questions 107
work pattern communication 251-253
work process 246-259
  starting a work process 256-259
work styles 209

_____ Please place me/us on your mailing list to receive announcements of audio tapes, modules, workbooks and other materials for continuing enrichment of my/our relationships.

_____ My partner and I are considering participation in a Couple Communication Group. Please send us the names of Certified Instructors in our area.

Name _____

Address _____

City _____ State _____ Zip Code _____

Occupation _____

DATE DUE

3 23 '88	
16 08 86	
JUN 29 84	

BRODART, INC.   Cat. No. 23-221